GIRLS' HANDBOOK

Uniform with this title
BOYS' HANDBOOK

SBN 361 03576 4
First published 1966
This completely revised edition published 1976 by
Purnell Books, Berkshire House, Queen Street,
Maidenhead, Berkshire
© 1976 Purnell & Sons Ltd.
Made and printed in Great Britain
by Purnell and Sons Ltd., Paulton (Bristol)
and London

Reprinted 1978

Girls' Handbook

New, revised edition

Purnell

Contents

Care of Your Pets   180

Sport   186

The Universe and Solar System

The Universe
No one knows how large the Universe may be, or even if it has a limit at all. The *visible* Universe (that is, the extent to which the largest telescope can penetrate) reaches out as much as 1,000 million light years away from Earth.

The Universe is made up of millions of Galaxies: each Galaxy is formed from millions of stars: the Sun is just one of the stars which belong to our own Galaxy.

Astronomical Distances
It would be impossible to talk of distances in the Universe in terms of kilometres. Instead, we refer to *light years* or the length of time which the light of a star takes to reach us. Light travels at a speed of 299,330 km. per second.

The light of the Moon reaches the Earth in $1\frac{1}{2}$ seconds.

The light of the Sun reaches the Earth in just over 8 min.

The nearest star is 4 light years away from us. The nearest Galaxy, the Andromeda Nebula, is 2 million light years away. The most distant bodies yet photographed are about 1,000 million light years away.

Another unit of distance is the *parsec*. One parsec equals 3.26 light years.

Planets of the Solar System

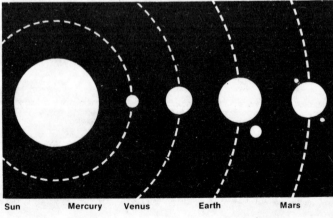

Sun   Mercury   Venus   Earth   Mars

The Solar System

The Sun is the centre of the Solar System and revolving around it are nine major *Planets*, of which the Earth is one. There are also many minor planets, called *Asteroids*, which are in orbit round the Sun. Each planet rotates on its own axis: the Earth, for example, takes one complete day to turn a full circle. The Sun also rotates on an axis: it takes between 25 and 27 Earth days to turn right round. The planets travel on fixed orbits round the Sun and the path taken by the Earth is known as the *ecliptic*. When the Earth has completed one orbit, a year has passed. Other members of the Solar System are *Comets*, which also travel round the Sun. Their orbits, however, are at all angles to the Earth's orbit and are highly eccentric, sometimes reaching far out into space. This is why a Comet is visible to Earth only at intervals and its appearance is often quite unexpected.

Planets of the Solar System

Name	No. of satellites	Diameter (in km.)	Kilometres from Sun	Orbital period	Length of "day"
Mercury	None	4,828	58 mill.	88 days	88 days
Venus	None	12,231	108 mill.	225 days	247 days
Earth	1 (moon)	12,757	150 mill.	1 year	23 hrs., 56 min.
Mars	2	6,759	228 mill.	1 year, 322 days	24 hrs., 37 min.
Jupiter	12	142,745	779 mill.	11 years, 315 days	9 hrs., 50 min.

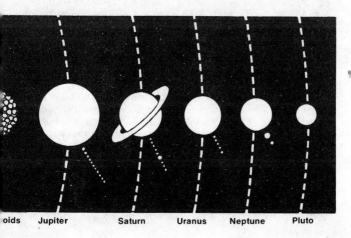

oids   Jupiter   Saturn   Uranus   Neptune   Pluto

Name	No. of satellites	Diameter (in km.)	Kilometres from Sun	Orbital period	Length of "day"
Saturn	9	120,858	1,427 mill.	29 years, 167 days	10 hrs., 14 min.
Uranus	5	49,727	2,871 mill.	84 years, 6 days	10 hrs., 49 min.
Neptune	2	53,108	4,498 mill.	164 years, 288 days	15 hrs., 40 min.
Pluto	None	Unknown	5,914 mill.	247 years, 255 days	6 days, 9 hrs., 17 min.

The Sun has a diameter of 1,390,470 km. Its satellites are those heavenly bodies that revolve around it, just as the Earth's satellite is the Moon, which revolves around the Earth.

The Moon has a diameter of 3,476 km. and it takes 27 days, 7 hours, 43 minutes to revolve around the Earth. Because it rotates in the same time as it revolves, it always presents nearly the same side of its surface to the Earth. Gravity on the Moon is much less than on Earth. Its landscape is rugged, with craggy mountain ranges and sharp craters. The speculation as to whether the Moon's surface was covered with a thick layer of dust was ended once and for all when Neil Armstrong and Edwin "Buzz" Aldrin became the first men on the Moon on July 20, 1969. There is dust on the Moon, certainly, but the surface is quite firm enough to bear the weight of spacecraft. The Moon is totally lacking in atmosphere, and moon-walkers have to wear space-suits. They also have to adapt their movements to the Moon's gravity, which is one-sixth that of Earth. So far, there have been ten astronauts on the Moon—Armstrong, Aldrin, Charles Conrad, Richard Gordon, Alan Shepard, Edgar Mitchell, David Scott, James Irwin, Charles Duke and John Young, all American.

In America, space exploration is carried out by the National Aeronautics and Space Administration (NASA), whose activities far exceed manned flights and moon-landings. In 1965, America's rocket, Mariner IV, passed close enough to Mars to send back photographs of the surface. The rocket's journey to Mars covered 523 million km. and took about eight months. This year, the Americans plan to use two Viking spacecraft to make soft-landings on Mars; these could be followed by manned journeys to Mars in the 1980's. In 1977, NASA hopes to send automated spacecraft even further afield—to Jupiter, Saturn and Pluto—while 1979 could see the launch of a robot craft to Jupiter, Uranus and Neptune.

Constellations
Constellations are groups of stars, which can be seen from the Northern Hemisphere and Southern Hemisphere. Many of the

Southern Constellations are visible from the Northern Hemisphere, and vice versa.

In the Northern Hemisphere

Andromeda	Chained Lady
Aries	Ram
Auriga	Charioteer
Boötes	Herdsman
Camelopardalis	Giraffe
Cancer	Crab
Canes Venatici	Hunting Dogs
Canis Minor	Lesser Dog
Cassiopeia	Lady in the Chair
Cepheus	Cassiopeia's Consort
Coma Berenices	Berenice's Hair
Corona Borealis	Northern Crown
Cygnus	Swan
Delphinus	Dolphin
Draco	Dragon
Equuleus	Lesser Horse
Gemini	Twins
Hercules	Legendary Strong Man
Lacerta	Lizard
Leo Minor	Lesser Lion
Lynx	Lynx
Lyra	Lyre
Pegasus	Winged Horse
Perseus	Legendary Hero
Sagitta	Arrow
Taurus	Bull
Triangulum	Triangle
Ursa Major	Great Bear
Ursa Minor	Little Bear
Vulpecula	Fox

In the Southern Hemisphere

Antlia	Pump
Apus	Bird of Paradise
Ara	Altar
Argo	Jason's Ship (divided into Carina, Puppis, Vela)
Caelum	Graving Tool
Canis Major	Greater Dog
Capricorn	Horned Goat
Carina	Keel (of the ship, Argo)
Centaurus	Centaur
Chamaeleon	Chameleon
Circinus	Pair of Compasses
Columba	Dove

Corona Australis	Southern Crown
Corvus	Crow
Crater	Cup
Crux	Southern Cross
Dorado	Goldfish
Eridanus	River
Fornax	Furnace
Grus	Crane
Horologium	Clock
Hydrus	Water Snake
Indus	Indian
Lepus	Hare
Libra	Scales
Lupus	Wolf
Mensa	Table Mountain
Microscopium	Microscope
Musca	Fly
Norma	Square
Octans	Octant
Pavo	Peacock
Phoenix	Phoenix
Pictor	Painter
Piscis Austrinus	Southern Fish
Puppis	Stern (of the ship, Argo)
Pyxis	Mariner's Compass (of Argo)
Reticulum	Net
Sagittarius	Archer
Scorpius	Scorpion
Sculptor	Sculptor
Scutum	Shield
Sextans	Sextant
Telescopium	Telescope
Triangulum Australe	Southern Triangle
Tucana	Toucan
Vela	Sails (of Argo)
Volans	Flying Fish

Both Northern and Southern

Aquarius	Water Carrier
Aquila	Eagle
Cetus	Sea Monster
Hydra	Sea Serpent
Leo	Lion
Monoceros	Unicorn
Ophiuchus	Serpent Holder
Orion	Giant Hunter
Pisces	Fishes
Serpens	Serpent
Sextans	Sextant
Virgo	Virgin

Brightest Stars

The brightness of stars is measured in magnitudes, with the first magnitude being brighter than the second and so on. Stars of the sixth magnitude are just visible to the naked eye, while the 508-cm. telescope, the world's largest, on Mount Palomar in California, U.S.A., can photograph stars of the 23rd magnitude. These are about 650 million times fainter than stars of the first magnitude. Four stars are so bright that they have to be given a minus magnitude. The 20 brightest stars are listed below.

Name	Constellation	Apparent magnitude	Distance from Earth (in light years)
Sirius A	Canis Major	—1.47	8.7
Canopus	Carina	—0.71	about 300
αCentauri	Centaurus	0.27	4.3
Vega	Lyra	0.03	26
Capella	Auriga	0.09	47
Arcturus	Boötes	0.06	36
Rigel	Orion	0.08	about 850
Procyon	Canis Minor	0.38	10.4
Achernar	Eridanus	0.49	75
βCentauri	Centaurus	0.61	300
Altair	Aquila	0.75	16
Betelgeuse	Orion (Ave)	0.92 (average)	650
αCrucis	Crux	0.80	270
Aldebaran	Taurus	0.78	65
Spica	Virgo	0.98	230
Antares	Scorpius	0.92	400
Pollux	Gemini	1.15	32
Fomalhaut	Piscis Austrinus	1.16	24
Deneb	Cygnus	1.26	1500
Regulus	Leo	1.33	85

The World—Part 1

Statistics of the Earth

Superficial area	509,805,240 sq. km.
Area of land	144,485,740 sq. km.
Area of water	365,319,500 sq. km.

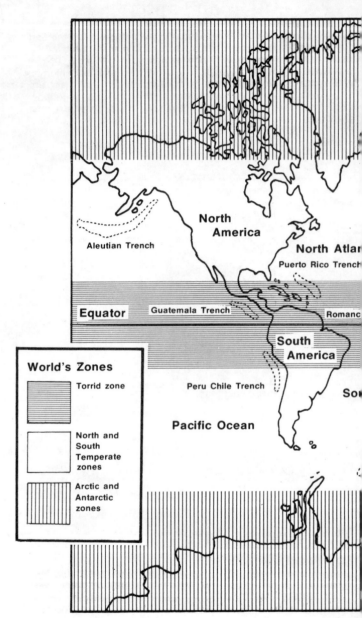

North America

Aleutian Trench

North Atlan

Puerto Rico Trench

Equator   Guatemala Trench

Romanc

South America

Peru Chile Trench

So

Pacific Ocean

World's Zones

Torrid zone

North and South Temperate zones

Arctic and Antarctic zones

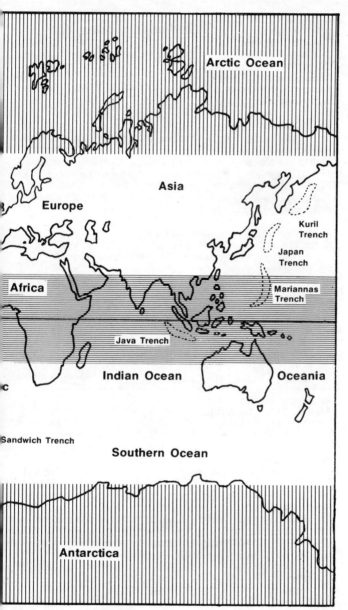

Arctic Ocean

Asia

Europe

Kuril
Trench

Japan
Trench

Africa

Mariannas
Trench

Java Trench

Indian Ocean

Oceania

Sandwich Trench

Southern Ocean

Antarctica

Estimated volume	1,065,599,171,700 cu. km.
Estimated weight	5,976 million million million tonnes
Diameter at Equator	12,756 km.
Diameter at Poles	12,715 km.
Circumference at Equator	40,075 km.
Circumference at Poles	40,008 km.
Speed of Earth revolving on axis	Over 1,609 km/h
Orbital speed round Sun	107,179 km/h

World Zones

There are five zones, calculated according to the average temperature at sea-level. The coldest zones are those nearest the Poles, the hottest are the zones near the Tropics of Capricorn and Cancer. Curiously enough, the Equator itself is not the hottest region. If you look at a globe, you will see that the deserts of the world lie approximately along the Tropics of Capricorn and Cancer. The five zones are:

Arctic	from North Pole	to 66° 30′ N.
North Temperate	from 66° 30′ N.	to 23° 38′ N.
Torrid	from 23° 38′ N.	to 23° 38′ S.
South Temperate	from 23° 38′ S.	to 66° 30′ S.
Antarctic	from 66° 30′ S.	to South Pole

Continents

The world's land area is divided into Continents. There are five of these—Asia, America, Africa, Antarctica and Europe—plus an area known as Oceania, which covers Australasia (Australia and New Zealand) and the non-Asian Pacific Islands.

Continent	Area in sq. km.
Asia (including the major part of the U.S.S.R.)	44,011,870
America (including North, Central and South America)	42,043,470
Africa	30,233,070
Antarctica	about 13,727,000
Europe (including that part of the U.S.S.R. west of the Ural Mountains)	10,523,170
Oceania	8,961,400

Oceans and Seas

There are only three Oceans, although the Arctic Sea is sometimes described as a fourth Ocean. The "Seven Seas", known to sailors of old, were the three principal Oceans divided into north and south and the Arctic Sea. Their areas are as follows:

Pacific	165,242,000 sq. km.
Atlantic	82,362,000 sq. km.

Indian	73,556,000 sq. km.
Arctic	13,986,000 sq. km.
Other Seas	25,511,500 sq. km.

Principal Seas	Area in sq. km.
Malay Sea	8,142,960
Caribbean Sea	2,753,170
Mediterranean Sea	2,503,882
Bering Sea	2,268,192
Gulf of Mexico	1,542,992
Sea of Okhotsk	1,527,582
East China Sea	1,249,157
Hudson Bay	1,232,322
Sea of Japan	1,007,510
Andaman Sea	797,720
North Sea	575,304
Black Sea	461,991
Red Sea	437,710
Baltic Sea	422,170
Persian Gulf	238,798
Gulf of St. Lawrence	237,762
English Channel and Irish Sea	178,451

Greatest Depths

Name	Location	Deepest point in m.
Mariana Trench	W. Pacific	11,033
Tonga-Kermadec Trench	S. Pacific	10,850
Philippine Trench	W. Pacific	10,539
Kuril-Kamchatka Trench	W. Pacific	10,382
Japan Trench	W. Pacific	10,375
Solomon Trench	S. Pacific	9,140
Puerto Rico Trench	W. Atlantic	8,382
South Sandwich Trench	S. Atlantic	8,264
Diamantina Trench	Indian Ocean	8,047
Yap Trench	W. Pacific	8,010
Peru-Chile Trench	E. Pacific	7,974
Aleutian Trench	N. Pacific	7,679
Romanche Trench	N-S Atlantic	7,635
Nansei Shoto Trench	W. Pacific	7,507
Cayman Trench	Caribbean	7,491
Java Trench	Indian Ocean	7,452
Guatemala Trench	E. Pacific	6,489
Yityaz Trench	S.W. Pacific	6,139

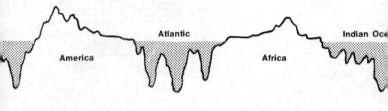

World's Largest Islands*

Name	Location	Area in sq. km.
Greenland	Arctic	2,142,707
New Guinea	Pacific	899,895
Borneo	Pacific	795,130
Baffin Island	Arctic	598,290
Madagascar	Indian	590,520
Sumatra	Indian	422,170
Great Britain	Atlantic	229,849
Honshu	Pacific	226,625
Celébes	Indian	189,070
Prince Albert	Arctic	155,400
South Island, N.Z.	Pacific	151,515
Java	Indian	125,356
North Island, N.Z.	Pacific	115,255
Cuba	Atlantic	113,960
Newfoundland	Atlantic	110,722
Luzon	Pacific	106,190
Ellesmere	Arctic	106,190
Iceland	Atlantic	103,600

World's Largest Peninsulas

Arabia	2,719,500 sq. km.
Southern India	2,072,000 sq. km.
Alaska	1,502,200 sq. km.
Labrador	1,295,000 sq. km.
Scandinavia	800,310 sq. km.
Iberian Peninsula	584,045 sq. km.

World's Highest Mountains

Name	Height in m.	Range	First climbed
Everest	8,840	Himalaya	May 29, 1953
K2	8,611	Karakoram	July 31, 1954
Kanchenjunga	8,579	Himalaya	May 25, 1955

*Australia (7,636,097 sq. km.) is regarded geographically as a continental land mass, not an island.

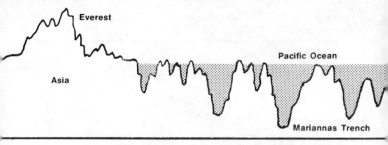

Name	Height in m.	Range	First climbed
Lhotse	8,501	Himalaya	May 18, 1956
Makalu	8,470	Himalaya	May 15, 1955
Dhaulagiri	8,167	Himalaya	May 13, 1960
Cho Oyu	8,153	Himalaya	Oct. 19, 1954
Nanga Parbat	8,126	Himalaya	July 3, 1953
Manaslu	8,125	Himalaya	May 9, 1956
Annapurna I	8,075	Himalaya	June 3, 1950
Gasherbrum I	8,068	Karakoram	July 5, 1958
Broad Peak	8,051	Karakoram	June 9, 1957
Gasherbrum II	8,034	Karakoram	July 7, 1956
Shisha Pangma	8,013	Himalaya	May 2, 1964
Gasherbrum III	7,952	Karakoram	Unclimbed
Annapurna II	7,937	Himalaya	May 17, 1960
Gasherbrum IV	7,925	Karakoram	Aug. 6, 1958

World's Principal Deserts

Sahara	3,367,000 sq. km.
Australian Desert	1,554,000 sq. km.
Arabian Desert	1,295,000 sq. km.
Gobi	1,036,000 sq. km.
Kalahari Desert	518,000 sq. km.

World's Most Notable Volcanoes

There are believed to be 535 active volcanoes, 80 of them under the sea. The main volcanic areas are around the shores of the North Pacific and the eastern shores of the South Pacific, the mid-Atlantic range, the Africa Rift Valley and from Greece and Turkey into Central Asia, the Himalayas and Assam. Volcanoes are classified as being extinct, dormant and active. Notable active volcanoes are:

Name	Height (in m.)	Range or location	Country	Last erupted
Lascar	5,990	Andes	Chile	1968

Name	Height (in m.)	Range or location	Country	Last erupted
Cotopaxi	5,897	Andes	Ecuador	1942
Popocatépetl	5,452	Altiplano de Mexico	Mexico	1920
Klyuchevskaya	4,750	Kamchatka Peninsula	U.S.S.R.	1966
Mauna Loa	4,170	Hawaii	U.S.A.	1950
*Erebus	3,795	Ross Is.	Antarctica	1947
Nyiragongo	3,470	Virunga	Zaire	1971

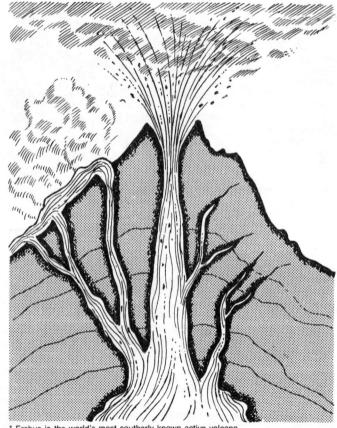

* Erebus is the world's most southerly known active volcano.

Name	Height (in m.)	Range or location	Country	Last erupted
Mt. Etna	3,263	Sicily	Italy	1974
The Peak	2,060	Tristan da Cunha	S. Atlantic	1961
Vesuvius	1,277	Bay of Naples	Italy	1944
Kilauea	1,247	Hawaii	U.S.A.	1971
Stromboli	925	Island	Mediterranean	1974
Helgafell	222	Westman Is.	Iceland	1973
Katmai	2,298	Alaska	U.S.A.	1931
Bezymianny	3,103	Kamchatka	U.S.S.R.	1970
Aso-San	1,602		Japan	1970
Fuji-San	3,798		Japan	1707
Mayon	2,435		Philippines	1969
Taal	3,045		Philippines	1969
Ngauruhoe	2,290		N. Zealand	1959
Tambora	2,868	Sunda Islands	Indonesia	1850
Pelee	1,397	Martinique	W. Indies	1929-32
Anak (New) Krakatau)	155	Island	Indonesia	1969

World's Deepest Caves

Name	Location	Depth in m.
Gouffre Berger	Isère, Grenoble, France	1,134
Mount Marquerais	France	777
Gouffre de la Pierre St. Martin	Basses-Pyrénées, France	728
Grotta della Piagga Bella	Piedmont border, Italy	689
Trou de Glaz	Isère, Grenoble, France	603
Abisso della Preta	Verona, Italy	594
Antro di Corchia	Tuscany, Italy	541
Abisso Vereo	Istria, Yugoslavia	539
Fledermaushöhle	Austria	539
Anou Boussouil	Djurdjura, Algeria	515

Kentucky, U.S.A., has the most extensive cave system. With 241 km. of passages, it is called the Mammoth Hole system. The U.S.A. can also claim the largest known cavern, the Big Room in the Carlsbad Caverns, New Mexico, which is 1,439 m. long, 200 m. wide and 100 m. high.

World's Longest Rivers

Name	Outflow	Length in km.
Nile	Mediterranean	6,695
Amazon	Atlantic	6,518

World's Longest Rivers

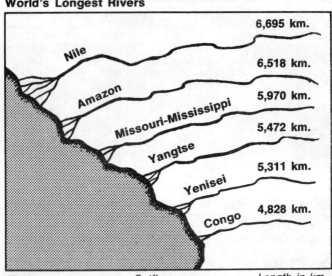

Name	Outflow	Length in km.
Missouri-Mississippi- Red Rock	Gulf of Mexico	5,970
Yangtse	North Pacific	5,472
Yenisei	Arctic Sea	5,311
Congo	Atlantic	4,828
Lena	Arctic Sea	4,506
Mekong	China Sea	4,506
Obi	Arctic Sea	4,345
Niger	Gulf of Guinea	4,184
Hwang Ho	North Pacific	4,184
Amur	North Pacific	4,023
Paranâ	Atlantic	3,943
Volga	Caspian Sea	3,862
Mackenzie	Beaufort Sea	3,701
Yukon	Bering Sea	3,219
Arkansas	Mississippi	3,219
Madeira	Amazon	3,219
Colorado	Gulf of California	3,219
St. Lawrence	Gulf of St. Lawrence	2,897
Rio Grande del Norte	Gulf of Mexico	2,897
São Francisco	Atlantic	2,897
Salween	Gulf of Martaban	2,897
Danube	Black Sea	2,776

Name	Outflow	Length in km.
Euphrates	Persian Gulf	2,736
Indus	Arabian Sea	2,736
Brahmaputra*	Bay of Bengal	2,704
Zambesi	Indian Ocean	2,628
Murray	Indian Ocean	2,589

World's Highest Waterfalls

Name	River	Location	Total drop in m.
Angel	Carrao	Venezuela	979
Tugela	Tugela	Natal, S. Africa.	948
Utigard	Jöstedal Glacier	Nesdel, Norway	800
Mongefossen	Monge	Mongebekk, Norway	774
Yosemite	Yosemite Creek	California, U.S.A.	739
Tyssestrengane	Tysso	Hardanger, Norway	646
Kukenaom	Arabopó	Venezuela	610

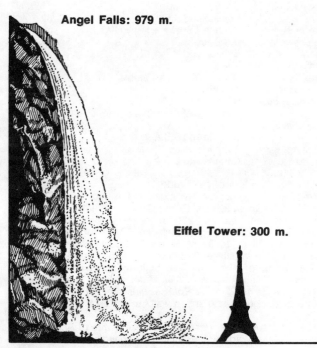

Angel Falls: 979 m.

Eiffel Tower: 300 m.

* Ganges (2,510 km. long) shares a delta with the Brahmaputra.

Name	River	Location	Total drop in m.
Sutherland	Arthur	S. Island, N. Zealand	581
Ribbon	Ribbon Fall Stream	California, U.S.A.	491
King George VI	Utshi	Guyana	488
Wollomombi	Wollomombi	Australia	481

Other falls are famous not for their height but for the volume of water which passes over them. Of these, Stanley Falls, part of the Congo River, have the biggest volume, some 16,990 cu. m. per second going over the Falls, yet their total drop is only 61 m. 1,058 cu. m. per second goes over the Victoria Falls (height: 108 m.) in the Zambesi River. The Niagara Falls on the border of U.S.A. and Canada carry 6,009 cu. m. of water per second. Their maximum height is 51 m.

World's Greatest Lakes

Name	Country	Area in sq. km.
Caspian Sea	U.S.S.R. and Iran	371,794
Superioi	Canada and U.S.A.	82,414
Victoria Nyanza	Uganda, Tanzania, Kenya	69,484
Aral'skoye More	U.S.S.R.	65,527
Huron	Canada and U.S.A.	59,596
Michigan	U.S.A.	58,016
Tanganyika	Congo, Tanzania, Zambia	32,893
Great Bear	Canada	31,792
Ozero Baykal	U.S.S.R.	30,510
Nyasa	Tanzania, Malawi, Mozambique	29,604
Great Slave	Canada	28,438
Erie	Canada and U.S.A.	25,719
Winnipeg	Canada	24,512
Ontario	Canada and U.S.A.	19,477

The Seven Wonders of the World

1. *The Pyramids of Egypt.* The oldest is the Pyramid of Zoser, at Saggara, built about 2,700 B.C. The Great Pyramid of Cheops was 147 m. high and measured 230 m. square at the base.

2. *The Hanging Gardens of Babylon.* These terraced gardens ranged from 23 m. to 91 m. above ground level and adjoined Nebuchadnezzar's palace, 96 km. south of Baghdad.

3. *The Tomb of Mausolus* was built by the widowed Queen Artemisia at Halicarnassus in Asia Minor about 350 B.C.

4. *The Temple of Diana at Ephesus* was erected in 350 B.C. in honour of the goddess Diana. It was burned by the Goths in A.D. 262.

5. *The Colossus of Rhodes* was a bronze statue of Apollo which stood astride the harbour entrance at the seaport of Rhodes. It was

The Pharos of Alexandria

Statue of Jupiter

Temple of Diana

Hanging Gardens

The Pyramids

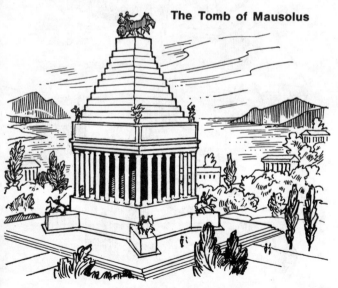

The Tomb of Mausolus

Colossus of Rhodes

erected around 280 B.C.

6. *The Statue of Jupiter Olympus.* Made of marble, inlaid with ivory and gold, by the sculptor, Phidias, about 430 B.C., the statue stood at Olympia in the plain of Ellis.

7. *The Pharos of Alexandria* was a marble watchtower and light-house on the island Pharos in the harbour of Alexandria.

The World—Part 2

The United Nations

The United Nations is the most important international organisation in existence. One of its principal aims is to maintain international peace and security, although other important facets of its work, carried out through organisations affiliated to the UN, include agricultural improvement, world health and education, economic development and finance.

The foundations of the organisation were laid at the Four-Nation Conference of Foreign Ministers, held at Moscow in 1943. The proposals were signed by the Foreign Ministers of Great Britain, U.S.A., U.S.S.R. and China. The structure of the UN was built at meetings held at Dumbarton Oaks, Washington, D.C., U.S.A., between August and October, 1944, discussed and criticised at San Francisco from April to June, 1945, by delegates from 50 nations, who put their signatures to the Charter, and came officially into existence on October 24, 1945. The UN's permanent headquarters are at Manhattan, New York.

Today, the UN has 135 member states. Their names are given below:

Name	Area in sq. km.	Population	Capital
Afghanistan	647,500	15,272,000	Kabul
Albania	27,713	1,965,000	Tirana
Algeria	2,217,040	15,000,000	Algiers
Argentina	2,797,200	23,364,000	Buenos Aires
Australia	7,687,120	13,026,000	Canberra
Austria	82,880	7,362,000	Vienna
Bahamas	13,934	169,000	Nassau

Name	Area in sq. km.	Population	Capital
Bahrain	552	216,000	Manama
Barbados	430	350,000	Bridgetown
Belgium	30,562	9,660,000	Brussels
Bhutan	46,620	800,000	Thimphu
Bolivia	1,074,850	4,334,000	La Paz
Botswana	28,946	648,000	Maseru
Brazil	8,518,510	100,000,000	Brasilia
Bulgaria	111,370	8,111,000	Sofia
Burma	678,580	28,201,000	Rangoon
Burundi	27,713	3,000,000	Bujumbura
*Byelorussia	207,200	9,003,000	Minsk
Cameroon	1,118,880	6,000,000	Yaoundé
Canada	9,220,400	21,568,000	Ottawa
Central African Republic	606,060	1,256,000	Bangui
Chad	1,263,920	2,755,000	Fort-Lamy
Chile	751,100	10,750,000	Santiago
China (Mainland)	11,137,000	700,000,000	Peking
Columbia	1,139,600	22,000,000	Bogotá
Congolese Republic	336,700	836,000	Leopoldville
Costa Rica	49,210	1,780,000	San José
Cuba	113,960	8,553,000	Havana
Cyprus	9,065	622,000	Nicosia
Czechoslovakia	139,860	14,000,000	Prague
Dahomey	121,730	2,203,000	Porto Novo
Denmark	42,994	4,960,000	Copenhagen
Dominican Republic	49,987	4,000,000	Santo Domingo
Ecuador	585,340	6,000,000	Quito
Egypt	999,740	34,840,000	Cairo
Equatorial Guinea	28,490	300,000	Santa Isabel
Ethiopia	1,036,000	24,320,000	Addis Ababa
Fiji	18,345	541,000	Suva
Finland	336,700	4,765,000	Helsinki
France	551,670	51,150,000	Paris
Gaboon	262,626	700,000	Libreville
Gambia	10,360	494,000	Bathurst
Germany, Democratic Republic of (East)	107,226	17,050,000	East Berlin
Germany, Federal Republic of (West)	248,640	61,690,000	Bonn
Ghana	238,280	8,546,000	Accra
Greece	132,090	8,900,000	Athens
Guatemala	108,780	5,200,000	Guatemala City
Guinea	251,230	3,920,000	Conakry
Guyana	214,970	740,000	Georgetown
Haiti	25,900	4,700,000	Port au Prince

Name	Area in sq. km.	Population	Capital
Honduras	111,370	2,690,000	Tegucigalpa
Hungary	93,240	10,420,000	Budapest
Iceland	104,895	208,000	Reykjavik
India	3,268,580	547,000,000	New Delhi
Indonesia	2,281,790	121,000,000	Djakarta
Iraq	445,486	8,262,000	Baghdad
Republic of Ireland	67,340	2,978,000	Dublin
Israel	20,720	3,001,000	Jerusalem
Italy	331,290	54,841,000	Rome
Ivory Coast	489,510	4,500,000	Abidjan
Jamaica	11,396	1,954,000	Kingston
Japan	370,370	107,332,000	Tokyo
Kenya	582,750	11,000,000	Nairobi
Khmer Republic (Cambodia)	181,300	7,000,000	Phnom Penh
Kuwait	15,022	733,200	Al Kuwait
Laos	233,100	3,000,000	Vientiane
Lebanon	11,137	2,700,000	Beirut
Lesotho	30,344	1,500,000	Mafeking
Liberia	111,370	1,650,000	Monrovia
Libya	2,097,900	2,000,000	Tripoli, Benghazi
Luxembourg	2,590	345,000	Luxembourg
Madagascar	590,520	7,000,000	Tananarive
Malawi	93,240	4,550,000	Zomba
Malaysia	334,110	10,811,000	Kuala Lumpur
Maldive Islands	298	114,000	Malé
Mali	1,204,350	5,000,000	Bamako
Malta	316	326,000	Valletta
Mauritania	833,980	1,170,000	Nouakchott
Mauritius	2,085	855,000	Port Louis
Mexico	1,963,220	50,000,000	Mexico City
Mongolia	1,554,000	1,300,000	Ulan Bator
Morocco	466,200	16,000,000	Rabat
Nepal	139,860	11,500,000	Katmandu
Netherlands	34,965	13,200,000	Amsterdam
New Zealand	269,360	2,809,000	Wellington
Nicaragua	147,630	1,984,000	Managua
Niger	1,253,560	4,016,000	Niamey
Nigeria	924,630	55,620,000	Lagos
Norway	323,750	3,950,000	Oslo
Oman	212,380	750,000	Muscat
Pakistan	803,944	64,890,000	Islamabad
Panama	82,621	1,425,000	Panama City
Paraguay	406,630	2,450,000	Asunción
Persia (Iran)	1,626,520	30,000,000	Tehran
Peru	1,375,290	13,600,000	Lima

Name	Area in sq. km.	Population	Capital
Philippines	297,850	37,500,000	Manila
Poland	313,390	32,486,000	Warsaw
Portugal	89,355	9,234,000	Lisbon
Qatar	10,360	130,000	Doba
Ruanda	25,900	3,000,000	Kigali
Rumania	237,244	20,420,000	Bucharest
Salvador	19,943	3,450,000	San Salvador
Saudi Arabia	2,400,930	6,000,000	Riyadh
Senegal	202,020	3,500,000	Dakar
Sierra Leone	72,520	2,500,000	Freetown
Singapore	583	2,167,000	Singapore
Somalia	637,140	2,930,000	Mogadishu
South Africa	1,105,930	21,558,000	Cape Town, Pretoria
South Yemen	160,295	1,300,000	Aden
Spain	510,230	33,960,000	Madrid
Sri Lanka (Ceylon)	64,750	12,748,000	Colombo
Sudan	2,530,430	16,000,000	Khartoum
Swaziland	17,353	465,000	Mbabane
Sweden	448,070	7,900,000	Stockholm
Syria	183,890	6,000,000	Damascus
Tanzania	888,370	12,250,000	Dar-es-Salaam
Thailand (Siam)	512,820	34,152,000	Bangkok
Togo	54,390	1,700,000	Lomé
Trinidad and Tobago	5,128	4,027,000	Port of Spain
Tunisia	116,550	5,200,000	Tunis
Turkey	764,050	35,600,000	Ankara
Uganda	243,460	9,660,000	Kampala
*Ukraine	600,880	47,900,000	Kiev
*U.S.S.R.	21,465,920	241,700,000	Moscow
United Arab Emirates	82,880	200,000	Abu Dhabi
United Kingdom	240,870	55,522,000	London
United States of America	9,204,860	208,439,000	Washington
Upper Volta	259,000	5,155,000	Ouagadougou
Uruguay	186,480	2,556,000	Montevideo
Venezuela	911,680	10,834,000	Caracas
Yemen	191,660	5,750,000	Sana, Taiz
Yugoslavia	256,410	21,022,000	Belgrade
Zaire	2,318,956	23,000,000	Kinshasa
Zambia	753,690	4,060,000	Lusaka

The following are independent countries of the world, which have not, so far, been admitted to membership of the United Nations:

*Byelorussia and the Ukraine are two republics of the U.S.S.R. but have separate membership.

Name	Area in sq. km.	Population	Capital
Andorra	466	20,550	Andorra La Vella
Bangladesh	142,776	75,000,000	Dacca
China (Taiwan)	35,742	14,781,000	Taipei
North Korea	124,320	6,500,000	Pyongyang
South Korea	95,830	31,139,000	Seoul
Liechtenstein	160	21,240	Vaduz
Monaco	1.3	23,600	Monaco
San Marino	59	19,000	San Marino
Switzerland	41,440	6,342,000	Berne
Vatican City State	44 hectares	1,000	Vatican City
Vietnam	332,556	42,300,000	Hanoi
Western Samoa	2,841	131,380	Apia

Principal Organs of the United Nations

1. *The General Assembly.* This consists of all the member nations, each of whom has up to five representatives but only one vote. There are seven main committees, on all of which every member has a right to be represented. They are: Political and Security; Economic and Financial; Social, Humanitarian and Culture; Trusteeship; Administrative and Budgetary; Legal; and Special Political.

2. *The Security Council.* There are 11 members of this Council, each with one representative and one vote. Five are permanent members—China, France, U.K., U.S.A. and U.S.S.R. The remaining six are elected for a two-year term. Except on procedural matters, an affirmative majority vote of seven members must include the five permanent members. It is this clause that makes the veto possible.

3. *The Economic and Social Council.* This is responsible under the General Assembly for carrying out the functions of the UN regarding social, cultural, educational and health matters.

4. *Trusteeship Council.* This was set up to administer certain territories which have been placed under UN supervision through individual Trusteeship Agreements.

5. *International Court of Justice.* The Court, which is the main judicial organ of the UN, is composed of 15 judges of different nations and meets at The Hague, Netherlands.

6. *The Secretariat.* This is the administrative section of the UN. Its principal officer is the Secretary-General, who is appointed by the General Assembly for a five-year term. Since 1946 there have been four Secretary-Generals. They are: Trygve Halvdan Lie (Norwegian): 1946 to 1952; Dag Hjalmar Agne Carl Hammarskjöld (Swedish): 1953 to 1961; U Thant (Burmese): 1961 to 1962 (acting), 1962 to 1971 (permanently); Kurt Waldheim (Austrian): 1971 to present day.

International Agencies

The following intergovernmental organisations come under the aegis of the United Nations:

International Labour Organisation (ILO). Established 1919. Linked with UN 1946. Headquarters: Geneva, Switzerland. Aims: to promote social justice and to improve labour conditions and living standards.

Food and Agriculture Organisation of the United Nations (FAO). Established 1945. Headquarters: Rome, Italy. Aims: to raise levels of nutrition and standards of living and to improve the production and distribution of agricultural products.

United Nations Educational, Scientific and Cultural Organisation (UNESCO). Established 1946. Headquarters: Paris, France. Aims: to promote collaboration among nations through education, science and culture, to further universal respect for justice, the rule of law and human rights, to advance the mutual knowledge and understanding of peoples, to maintain, increase and diffuse knowledge.

World Health Organisation (WHO). Established 1948. Headquarters: Geneva. Aims: to spread knowledge, train personnel and assist countries in their fight against disease.

International Bank for Reconstruction and Development (The World Bank). Established 1945. Headquarters: Washington, D.C., U.S.A. Aims: to assist in the development of territories by aiding capital investment.

International Development Association (IDA). Established 1960 and affiliated to the World Bank. Headquarters: Washington, D.C. Aims: to make special loans to the under-developed countries.

International Finance Corporation (IFC). Established 1956. Headquarters: Washington, D.C. Aims: to assist industrial development of poorer countries by stimulating the flow of capital investment.

International Monetary Fund (IMF). Established 1945. Headquarters: Washington, D.C. Aims: to promote international monetary cooperation and the expansion of international trade.

International Civil Aviation Organisation (ICAO). Established 1947. Headquarters: Montreal, Canada. Aims: to establish international standards and regulations for civil aviation and to encourage safety measures and co-operation between nations.

Universal Postal Union (UPU). Established 1848. Linked with UN 1948. Headquarters: Berne, Switzerland. Aims: to form a single postal territory in which all nations agree to transmit the mail of other countries by the best means.

International Telecommunication Union (ITU). Established 1865. Headquarters: Geneva. Aims: to develop and standardise telegraph, telephone and radio services throughout the world.

World Meteorological Organisation (WMO). Established 1950. Headquarters: Geneva. Aims: to promote, standardise and publish meteorological observations particularly as a means of benefiting aviation, shipping, and agriculture, etc.

Intergovernmental Maritime Consultative Organisation (IMCO). Established 1958. Headquarters: London. Aims: to promote co-operation among governments in all matters concerning shipping, especially safety at sea.

International Trade. A draft charter of an international trade organisation was completed in 1948 but such an organisation has not yet been established. However, more than 60 countries are parties to the General Agreement on Tariffs and Trade, which was signed in 1947. The aims of GATT are to lower and stabilise tariffs, expand international trade and promote economic development.

World's Largest Cities

Name	Country	Population
Tokyo	Japan	11,454,000
*Shanghai	China	10,820,000
*London	England	8,186,830
*New York	U.S.A.	7,895,600
Peking	China	7,570,000
Moscow	U.S.S.R.	7,050,000
Mexico City	Mexico	7,005,855
*Bombay	India	5,968,546
Sao Paulo	Brazil	5,901,533
Seoul	South Korea	5,536,377
*Djakarta	Indonesia	4,576,000
*Rio de Janeiro	Brazil	4,296,782
Tientsin	China	4,280,000
*Leningrad	U.S.S.R.	3,607,000
Chicago	U.S.A.	3,550,404
*Calcutta	India	3,439,887
Berlin (East and West)	G.D.R. (E. Germany) (West Berlin is a self-governing political unit)	3,400,228
Cairo	Egypt	3,346,000
Delhi	India	3,279,955
Madrid	Spain	3,146,071
*Osaka	Japan	2,980,487
*Buenos Aires	Argentina	2,972,000
*Los Angeles	U.S.A.	2,894,911
*Sydney	Australia	2,807,828
Rome	Italy	2,755,135
Paris	France	2,607,625
Shenyang	China	2,411,000
Wuhan	China	2,146,000
*Bangkok	Thailand	2,138,000

World's Tallest Buildings

Name	City	No. of storeys	Height in m.
Empire State Building	New York	102	449

* Seaport

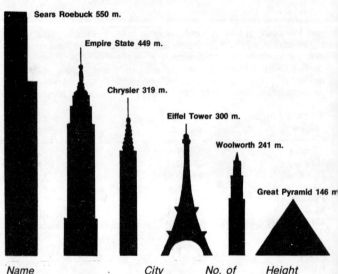

Sears Roebuck 550 m.
Empire State 449 m.
Chrysler 319 m.
Eiffel Tower 300 m.
Woolworth 241 m.
Great Pyramid 146 m

Name	City	No. of storeys	Height in m.
World Trade Centre	New York	110	412
Chrysler Building	New York	77	319
60 Wall Tower	New York	67	289
Bank of Manhattan	New York	71	274
R.C.A. Building	New York	70	259
Chase Manhattan Building	New York	60	248
Pan American Building	New York	60	246
Woolworth Building	New York	59	241
Mikhail Lomonosov University Building	Moscow	28	240
Palace of Culture and Science	Warsaw	33	230

World's Longest Bridge Spans

Name	Location	Length in m.
Verrazano-Narrows	Brooklyn—Staten Is., U.S.A.	1,298
Golden Gate	San Francisco Bay, U.S.A.	1,280
Mackinac	Straits of Mackinac, Michigan, U.S.A.	1,158
George Washington	Hudson River, New York City, U.S.A.	1,067

Verrazano Narrows, USA   1,298 m.

Quebec Railway Bridge, Canada   549 m.

Sydney Harbour Bridge, Australia   503 m.

Name	Location	Length in m.
Tagus	Lisbon, Portugal	1,011
Firth of Forth	Firth of Forth, Scotland	1,006
Severn	Severn Estuary, England	987
Tacoma Narrows	Washington, U.S.A.	853

Note: all these bridges are suspension construction.

World's Longest Tunnels

Name	Place	Length in km.
Simplon	Brigue, Switzerland, to Iselle, Italy	19.83
Apennine	North of Vernio, Italy	18.49
St. Gotthard	Göschenen to Airolo, Switzerland	14.90
Lötschberg	Kandersteg to Goppenstein, Switzerland	14.53
Hokurika	Tsuruga to Imajō, Japan	13.86
Fréjus	Modane, France, to Bardonecchia, Italy	12.84
Cascade	Berne-Scenic, Washington, U.S.A.	12.52
Arlberg	Langen to St. Anton, Austria	10.30

World's Largest Passenger Liners

Name	Nationality	Gross Regis- tered Tonnage
France	French	66,348
Queen Elizabeth 2	British	65,863
United States	American	52,072
Canberra	British	45,733
Michelangelo	Italian	43,000
Raffaello	Italian	43,000
Oriana	British	41,915
Rotterdam	Dutch	38,645
Windsor Castle	British	37,640
Nieuw Amsterdam	Dutch	36,982
Mauretania	British	35,674
Coronia	British	34,172

Countries of the World

This section does not include the members of the British Commonwealth, which can be found in the next chapter.

Afghanistan
Principal languages: Pakhto (Pushtu) and Dari Persian.
Principal religion: Islamic.
Head of State: King.
Currency: Afghani.
Flag: Vertical stripes of black, red and green, with white device in centre.

Albania
Principal language: Shgyp.
Principal religion: Islamic.
Head of State: President of the Presidium of the People's Assembly.
Currency: Lek.
Flag: Black two-headed eagle, surmounted by yellow-edged red star, all on a red background.

Algeria
Principal languages: Arabic and French.
Principal religion: Islamic.
Head of State: President.
Currency: Dinar.
Flag: Vertical stripes of black, red and green, with white ground.

Andorra
Principal languages: Catalán, Spanish and French.
Principal religion: Roman Catholic.
Head of State: Co-princes (The Bishop of Urgel and the President of France).
Currency: French franc and Spanish peseta.
Flag: Vertical bands of blue, yellow and red. The yellow band in the centre sometimes bears the Andorran coat of arms.

Argentina
Principal language: Spanish.
Principal religion: Roman Catholic.
Head of State: President.
Currency: Peso.
Flag: Three horizontal bands, blue, white, blue, with rising sun on
    white band.
Austria
Principal language: German.
Principal religion: Roman Catholic.
Head of State: President.
Currency: Schilling.
Flag: Horizontal stripes of red, white, red, with eagle crest on white
    stripe.
Bahrain
Principal language: Arabic.
Principal religion: Islamic.
Head of State: Shaikh.
Currency: Persian Gulf Indian rupee.
Flag: Red, with vertical straight or serrated white bar next to staff.
Belgium
Principal languages: Flemish and French.
Principal religion: Roman Catholic.
Head of State: King.
Currency: Franc.
Flag: Vertical stripes of black, yellow, red.
Bhutan
Principal language: Dzongkha.
Principal religions: Shintō, Buddhism.
Head of State: King.
Currency: Indian rupee.
Flag: Orange-yellow and crimson, divided diagonally from bottom
    left to top right, with white wingless dragon superimposed.
Bolivia
Principal languages: Spanish, Indian languages.
Principal religion: Roman Catholic.
Head of State: Co-Presidents of Military Junta.
Currency: Bolivian peso.
Flag: Three horizontal bands of red, yellow, green, with device on
    yellow band.
Brazil
Principal language: Portuguese.
Principal religion: Roman Catholic.
Head of State: President.
Currency: Cruzeiro.
Flag: Green, with yellow diamond in centre. Blue sphere with white
    band and stars in centre of diamond.
Bulgaria
Principal languages: Bulgarian, Turkish.

39

Principal religion: Eastern Orthodox.
Head of State: President of the Presidium of the National Assembly.
Currency: Ley.
Flag: Three horizontal bands of white, green, red, with national emblem on white stripe near hoist.

Burma
Principal language: Burmese.
Principal religion: Buddhism.
Head of State: Chairman of Revolutionary Government.
Currency: Kyat.
Flag: Red, with blue canton bearing large white star surrounded by five smaller stars.

Burundi
Principal languages: Bantu dialects and French.
Principal religions: Animism and Roman Catholic.
Head of State: King (Mwami).
Currency: Ruanda and Burundi franc.
Flag: White diagonal cross on green and red quarters, with white panel in centre enclosing drum and ear of sorghum.

Cameroon
Principal language: French.
Principal religion: Animism.
Head of State: President.
Currency: Franc de la Communauté Financière Africaine (Franc C.F.A.).
Flag: Vertical stripes of green, red and yellow, with two stars in upper half of green band.

Central African Republic
Principal languages: French, Sango dialect.
Principal religions: Animism, Christianity.
Head of State: President.
Currency: Franc C.F.A.
Flag: Four horizontal stripes of blue, white, yellow, green, crossed by red vertical stripe. Yellow star in centre of blue stripe next to staff.

Chad
Principal language: French.
Principal religion: Islamic.
Head of State: President.
Currency: Franc C.F.A.
Flag: Vertical stripes of blue, yellow and red.

Chile
Principal language: Spanish.
Principal religion: Roman Catholic.
Head of State: President.
Currency: Escudo.
Flag: Two horizontal bands of red and white. White star on blue square next to staff.

China (The People's Republic)

Principal language: Northern Chinese.
Principal religions: Confucianism, Taoism, Buddhism.
Head of State: Chairman.
Currency: People's Bank yuan.
Flag: Red, with large gold star and arc of smaller stars in upper hoist.

China (Taiwan)
Principal language: Northern Chinese.
Principal religion: Buddhism.
Head of State: President.
Currency: New Taiwan dollar.
Flag; Red, with blue quarter containing white sun.

Colombia
Principal language: Spanish.
Principal religion: Roman Catholic.
Head of State: President.
Currency: Peso.
Flag: Broad yellow band in upper half, above equal bands of blue and red.

Congo (Now called Zaire)
Principal languages: French, Bantu languages.
Principal religions: Animism, Roman Catholic.
Head of State: President.
Currency: Franc C.F.A.
Flag: Green and red triangles divided by yellow stripe.

Congolese Republic (Leopoldville)
Principal languages: Kiswahili, Tshiluba, Lingala Kikongo.
Principal religions: Animism, Roman Catholic.
Head of State: President.
Currency: Congolese franc.
Flag: Blue, with diagonal red band, flanked by yellow stripes. Yellow star next to staff.

Costa Rica
Principal language: Spanish.
Principal religion: Roman Catholic.
Head of State: President.
Currency: Colón.
Flag: Five horizontal stripes in blue, white, red, white, blue. The red is twice as wide as the others and bears an emblem near the staff.

Cuba
Principal language: Spanish.
Principal religion: Roman Catholic.
Head of State: President.
Currency: Peso.
Flag: Five horizontal bands, blue, white, blue, white, blue. Red triangle at hoist, charged with silver star.

Czechoslovakia
Principal languages: Czech, Slovak.

Principal religion: Roman Catholic.
Head of State: President.
Currency: Koruna.
Flag: White and red horizontal stripes, blue triangle next to staff.

Dahomey
Principal language: French.
Principal religion: Animism.
Head of State: President.
Currency: Franc C.F.A.
Flag: Three stripes, one green (vertical), two yellow and red (horizontal).

Denmark
Principal language: Danish.
Principal religion: Danish Lutheran Church.
Head of State: King.
Currency: Krone.
Flag: Red, with white cross.

Dominican Republic
Principal language: Spanish.
Principal religion: Roman Catholic.
Head of State: President.
Currency: Dominican Republic peso.
Flag: Red and blue, with white cross bearing emblem at centre.

Ecuador
Principal languages: Spanish, Quéchua, Jíbaro.
Principal religion: Roman Catholic.
Head of State: President.
Currency: Sucre.
Flag: Three horizontal bands, yellow, blue, red. Yellow twice as wide as others and bearing emblem in centre.

Egypt
Principal languages: Arabic, English, French.
Principal religion: Islamic.
Head of State: President.
Currency: Egyptian pound.
Flag: Horizontal bands of red, white, black, with two green stars in white band.

Equatorial Guinea
Principal language: Spanish.
Principal religion: Roman Catholic.
Head of State: President.
Currency: Peseta.
Flag: Three horizontal bands, green over white over red. Blue triangle next to staff.

Ethiopia
Principal language: Amharic.
Principal religions: Ethiopian Orthodox Church, Islamic.
Head of State: Emperor.
Currency: Ethiopian dollar.

Flag: Three horizontal bands, green, yellow, red. Crowned lion at centre.

Finland

Principal language: Finnish.

Principal religion: Evangelical Lutheran Church.

Head of State: President.

Currency: Finnmark.

Flag: White with blue cross.

France

Principal language: French.

Principal religion: Roman Catholic.

Head of State: President.

Currency: Franc.

Flag: "Tricolour". Three vertical bands, blue, white, red. Blue next to staff.

Gabon

Principal language: French.

Principal religions: Christianity, Animism.

Head of State: President.

Currency: Franc C.F.A.

Flag: Horizontal bands, green, yellow, blue.

Germany (East)

Principal language: German.

Principal religion: Protestant.

Head of State: Chairman of the Council of States.

Currency: Mark.

Flag: Black, red, gold horizontal bands. Coat of arms in centre.

Germany (West)

Principal language: German.

Principal religions: Protestant, Roman Catholic.

Head of State: President.

Currency: Deutsche Mark.

Flag: Horizontal bars of black, red, gold.

Greece

Principal language: Greek.

Principal religion: Greek Orthodox Church.

Head of State: President.

Currency: Drachma.

Flag: Nine horizontal bands of blue and white, alternating, with white cross on blue ground in corner.

Guatemala

Principal languages: Spanish, Quiché.

Principal religion: Roman Catholic.

Head of State: President.

Currency: Quetzal.

Flag: Three vertical bands, blue, white, blue. Coat of arms on white stripe.

Guinea

Principal languages: French, Fulani.

Principal religions: Islamic, Animism.
Head of State: President.
Currency: Guinean franc.
Flag: Three vertical stripes, red, yellow, green.

Haiti

Principal languages: French, Creole.
Principal religions: Roman Catholic, Voodoo.
Head of State: President.
Currency: Gourde.
Flag: Two vertical bands, black (next to hoist), red.

Honduras

Principal language: Spanish.
Principal religion: Roman Catholic.
Head of State: President.
Currency: Lempira.
Flag: Three horizontal bands, blue, white, blue, with five blue stars on white band.

Hungary

Principal language: Magyar.
Principal religion: Roman Catholic.
Head of State: President.
Currency: Forint.
Flag: Horizontal bands of red, white, green.

Iceland

Principal language: Icelandic.
Principal religion: Evangelical Lutheran Church.
Head of State: President.
Currency: Krónur.
Flag: Blue, with white-bordered red cross.

Indonesia

Principal languages: Bahasa Indonesia (Malay), Javanese.
Principal religion: Islamic.
Head of State: President.
Currency: Rupiah.
Flag: Two equal bands of red over white.

Iran (Persia)

Principal languages: Persian, Kurdish.
Principal religion: Islamic.
Head of State: Shahanshah.
Currency: Rial.
Flag: Equal horizontal bands, green, white, red, with arms (lion and sun) in centre.

Iraq

Principal language: Arabic.
Principal religion: Islamic.
Head of State: President.
Currency: Iraqi dinar.
Flag: Horizontal stripes, red, white, black, with three green stars on white stripe.

Ireland (Eire)
Principal language: English.
Principal religion: Roman Catholic.
Head of State: President.
Currency: Irish pound.
Flag: Equal vertical stripes, green, white, orange.
Israel
Principal languages: Modern Hebrew, Arabic.
Principal religion: Judaism.
Head of State: President.
Currency: Israeli pound.
Flag: White, with two horizontal blue stripes and Shield of David in
    centre.
Italy
Principal language: Italian.
Principal religion: Roman Catholic.
Head of State: President.
Currency: Lira.
Flag: Vertical stripes of green, white, red.
Ivory Coast
Principal language: French.
Principal religion: Animism.
Head of State: President.
Currency: Franc C.F.A.
Flag: Three vertical stripes, orange, white, green.
Japan
Principal languages: Japanese, Ainu.
Principal religions: Mahāyāna, Buddhism.
Head of State: Emperor.
Currency: Yen.
Flag: White, with red sun in centre.
Jordan
Principal language: Arabic.
Principal religion: Islamic.
Head of State: King.
Currency: Dinar.
Flag: Black, white, green horizontal stripes, with red triangle at
    hoist containing white star.
Khmer Republic (formerly Cambodia)
Principal language: Khmer.
Principal religion: Hinayana Buddhism.
Head of State: President.
Currency: Riel.
Flag: Horizontal stripes of blue, red (wide), blue with white
    emblem in centre.
Korea (North)
Principal language: Korean.
Principal religions: Buddhism, Confucianism, Taoism.
Head of State: Chairman of the Presidium of the Supreme People's

Assembly.

Currency: Won.

Flag: Red, with blue stripes at upper and lower edges, each separated from red by white stripe. Flag bears white disc containing red star.

Korea (South)

Principal language: Korean.

Principal religions: Mahayana Buddhism, Confucianism, Taoism.

Head of State: President.

Currency: Won.

Flag: White, with red and blue disc in centre and parallel black bars in each corner.

Kuwait

Principal language: Arabic.

Principal religion: Islamic.

Head of State: Amir.

Currency: Kuwait dinar.

Flag: Three horizontal stripes of green, white, red, with black trapezoid next to staff.

Laos

Principal language: Lao.

Principal religion: Hinayana Buddhism.

Head of State: King.

Currency: Kip.

Flag: Red, with three-headed white elephant on five steps, surmounted by parasol.

Lebanon

Principal languages: Arabic, Armenian.

Principal religions: Christianity, Islamic.

Head of State: President.

Currency: Lebanese pound.

Flag: Horizontal bands of red, white, red, with green cedar of Lebanon in centre of white band.

Liberia

Principal language: English.

Principal religions: Methodism, other Protestant, Animism.

Head of State: President.

Currency: Liberian dollar.

Flag: Horizontal stripes (11) of white and red, with white star on blue ground next to flagstaff.

Libya

Principal language: Arabic.

Principal religion: Islamic.

Head of State: King.

Currency: Libyan pound.

Flag: Red, black, green horizontal stripes, with white crescent and star in centre.

Liechtenstein

Principal language: German.

Principal religion: Roman Catholic.
Head of State: Prince.
Currency: Swiss franc.
Flag: Blue and red, with gold crown on the blue part.

Luxemburg
Principal languages: Letzeburgesch, French, German.
Principal religion: Roman Catholic.
Head of State: Grand Duke.
Currency: Luxemburg franc.
Flag: Three horizontal bands, red, white, blue.

Madagascar
Principal languages: Malagasy, Hova, French.
Principal religions: Animism, Christianity.
Head of State: President.
Currency: Malagasy franc.
Flag: Horizontal bands of red, green, with vertical white band by staff.

Maldive Islands
Principal languages: Maldivian, Arabic.
Principal religion: Islamic.
Head of State: Sultan.
Currency: Maldivian rupee.
Flag: Green, with broad red border and white crescent at centre.

Mali
Principal languages: French, Tekrourian, Mande.
Principal religions: Islamic and Animism.
Head of State: President.
Currency: Mali franc.
Flag: Vertical stripes of green, yellow, red.

Mauritania
Principal languages: French, Arabic, Hassaniya.
Principal religion: Islamic.
Head of State: President.
Currency: Franc C.F.A.
Flag: Yellow star and crescent on green ground.

Mexico
Principal language: Spanish.
Principal religion: Roman Catholic.
Head of State: President.
Currency: Peso.
Flag: Three vertical bands, green, white, red, with shield of Mexico in centre.

Monaco
Principal language: French.
Principal religion: Roman Catholic.
Head of State: Prince.
Currency: Franc.
Flag: Red and white horizontal bands.

Mongolia

Principal language: Mongolian.
Principal religion: Buddhist Lamaism.
Head of State: Prime Minister.
Currency: Tughrik.
Flag: Vertical stripes, red, blue, red, with gold Soyombo symbol in left-hand stripe.

Morocco
Principal languages: Arabic, Berber.
Principal religion: Islamic.
Head of State: King.
Currency: Dirham.
Flag: Red, with green Seal of Solomon in centre.

Nepal
Principal language: Nepáli.
Principal religions: Hinduism, Buddhism.
Head of State: King.
Currency: Nepalese rupee.
Flag: Two crimson pennants, each with blue border. White crescent moon in top pennant, white sun in lower.

Netherlands
Principal language: Dutch.
Principal religions: Roman Catholic, Dutch Reformed Church.
Head of State: Queen.
Currency: Florin or guilder.
Flag: Three horizontal bands of red, white and blue.

Nicaragua
Principal language: Spanish.
Principal religion: Roman Catholic.
Head of State: President.
Currency: Córdoba.
Flag: Three horizontal bands, blue, white, blue. Coat of arms on white band.

Niger
Principal languages: French, Taurecheg, Poular, Haouassa.
Principal religions: Islamic, Animism, Christianity.
Head of State: President.
Currency: Franc C.F.A.
Flag: Three horizontal stripes, orange, white, green, with orange disc in centre of white stripe.

Norway
Principal languages: Norwegian, Lapp.
Principal religion: Evangelical Lutheran Church.
Head of State: King.
Currency: Norwegian krone.
Flag: Red, with white-bordered blue cross.

Oman
Principal language: Arabic.
Principal religion: Islamic.
Head of State: Sultan.

48

Currency: Persian Gulf Indian rupee (on coast)
Maria Theresa dollar (interior).
Flag: White and green horizontal bands divided by thin red band.
Vertical red band near staff, with white symbol in upper half.
Pakistan
Principal language: Urdu.
Principal religion: Moslem.
Head of State: President.
Currency: Rupee.
Flag: Dark green, with white vertical stripe at staff, white crescent
and star.
Panama
Principal language: Spanish.
Principal religion: Roman Catholic.
Head of State: President.
Currency: Balboa.
Flag: Quartered red, white (two), blue. White quarters bear blue star
in one, red star in other.
Paraguay
Principal languages: Spanish, Guaraní.
Principal religion: Roman Catholic.
Head of State: President.
Currency: Guaraní.
Flag: Three horizontal bands, red, white, blue with national seal on
obverse white band. Treasury seal on reverse white band.
Peru
Principal languages: Spanish, Quechua, Aymará.
Principal religion: Roman Catholic.
Head of State: President.
Currency: Sol.
Flag: Three vertical bands, red, white, red. Coat of arms on white
band.
Philippines
Principal languages: Filipino, English, Spanish.
Principal religion: Roman Catholic.
Head of State: President.
Currency: Peso.
Flag: Two equal horizontal bands of blue and red. Gold sun with
three stars on a white triangle next to staff.
Poland
Principal language: Polish.
Principal religion: Roman Catholic.
Head of State: Chairman of the Council of State.
Currency: Zloty.
Flag: Two equal horizontal bands, white and red.
Portugal
Principal language: Portuguese.
Principal religion: Roman Catholic.
Head of State: President.

Currency: Escudo.
Flag: Green and red, with arms in centre.
Qatar
Principal language: Arabic.
Principal religion: Islamic.
Head of State: Shaikh.
Currency: Persian Gulf Indian rupee.
Flag: White, coffee, divided by serrated vertical line.
Ruanda
Principal languages: French, Hutu.
Principal religions: Christianity, Animism.
Head of State: President.
Currency: Ruanda-Burundi franc.
Flag: Three vertical bands, red, yellow, green, with letter R on yellow band.
Rumania
Principal language: Rumanian.
Principal religion: Rumanian Orthodox Church.
Head of State: President.
Currency: Leu.
Flag: Three vertical bands, blue, yellow, red, with national emblem in centre.
Salvador
Principal language: Spanish.
Principal religion: Roman Catholic.
Head of State: President.
Currency: Colón.
Flag: Three horizontal bands, light blue, white, light blue, with coat of arms on white band.
San Marino
Principal language: Italian.
Principal religion: Roman Catholic.
Head of State: Two regents, elected every six months.
Currency: Italian lira.
Flag: Two horizontal bands, white, blue, with coat of arms in centre.
Saudi Arabia
Principal language: Arabic.
Principal religion: Islamic.
Head of State: King.
Currency: Riyal.
Flag: Green, white Arabic device in centre, white scimitar below.
Senegal
Principal language: French.
Principal religion: Islamic.
Head of State: President.
Currency: Franc C.F.A.
Flag: Three vertical bands, green, yellow, red. Green star on yellow band.
Somalia

Principal languages: Somali, Arabic, Italian, English.
Principal religion: Islamic.
Head of State: President.
Currency: Somalo.
Flag: White star on pale blue ground.
South Africa
Principal languages: Africaans, English.
Principal religion: Dutch Reformed Church.
Head of State: President.
Currency: Rand.
Flag: Three horizontal bands of orange, white, blue. In centre, three small flags; Union Jack, old Orange Free State flag and old Transvaal Vierkleur.
Spain
Principal languages: Spanish, Catalán, Basque.
Principal religion: Roman Catholic.
Head of State: King.
Currency: Peseta.
Flag: Three horizontal bands, red, yellow, red, with coat of arms on yellow band.
Sudan
Principal language: Arabic.
Principal religion: Islamic.
Head of State: President.
Currency: Sudanese pound.
Flag: Three horizontal stripes, blue, yellow, green.
Sweden
Principal language: Swedish.
Principal religion: Evangelical Lutheran Church.
Head of State: King.
Currency: Krona.
Flag: Yellow cross on blue ground.
Switzerland
Principal languages: German, French, Italian.
Principal religions: Protestant, Roman Catholic.
Head of State: President (elected yearly).
Currency: Swiss franc.
Flag: Red with white cross.
Syria
Principal language: Arabic.
Principal religion: Islamic.
Head of State: President.
Currency: Syrian pound.
Flag: Red, white, black horizontal bands, with three green stars on central white band.
Thailand (Siam)
Principal language: Thai.
Principal religion: Hinayana Buddhism.
Head of State: King.

Currency: Baht.

Flag: Five horizontal bands, red, white, dark blue, white, red. Blue band twice as wide as others.

Togo

Principal languages: French, Ewê, Kabra, Hausa.

Principal religions: Animism, Christianity.

Head of State: President.

Currency: Franc C.F.A.

Flag: Five alternating green and yellow horizontal stripes. Red quarter near staff bears white star.

Tunisia

Principal languages: Arabic, French.

Principal religion: Islamic.

Head of State: President.

Currency: Dinar.

Flag: Red crescent and star in white orb on red ground.

Turkey

Principal language: Turkish.

Principal religion: Islamic.

Head of State: President.

Currency: Turkish pound.

Flag: Red, with white crescent and star.

Union of Soviet Socialist Republics (U.S.S.R.)

Principal language: Russian.

Principal religion: No state religion.

Head of State: Chairman of the Presidium of the Supreme Soviet.

Currency: Rouble.

Flag: Star, hammer and sickle on red ground.

United Arab Emirates (Trucial States)

Principal language: Arabic.

Principal religion: Islamic.

Head of State: President.

Currency: Qatar/Dubai riyal.

Flag: Three horizontal bands, green, white and black. Red vertical stripe near staff.

United States of America

Principal language: English.

Principal religions: Baptist, Methodist, Roman Catholic.

Head of State: President.

Currency: Dollar.

Flag: Thirteen red and white horizontal stripes (representing the original States of the Union) with fifty white stars (representing the present fifty States) on a blue ground at the upper hoist. The flag is popularly known as the "Stars and Stripes" or "Old Glory".

Upper Volta

Principal language: French.

Principal religion: Animism.

Head of State: President.

Currency: Franc C.F.A.
Flag: Three horizontal stripes, black, white, red.

Uruguay
Principal language: Spanish.
Principal religion: Roman Catholic.
Head of State: President.
Currency: Peso.
Flag: Four blue and five white horizontal stripes, with white square bearing gold sun near staff.

Vatican City
Principal language: Italian.
Principal religion: Catholic.
Head of State: Pope.
Currency: Italian lira.
Flag: Yellow and white vertical stripes, with crest showing crossed keys and triple crown of the Pope.

Venezuela
Principal language: Spanish.
Principal religion: Roman Catholic.
Head of State: President.
Currency: Bolivar.
Flag: Three horizontal bands, yellow, blue, red, with seven white stars on blue band and crest next to staff on yellow band.

Vietnam (North)
Principal language: Vietnamese.
Principal religions: Buddhism, Taoism, Confucianism.
Head of State: President.
Currency: Dong.
Flag: Red, with yellow star in centre.

Vietnam (South)
Principal language: Vietnamese.
Principal religions: Buddhism, Taoism.
Head of State: President.
Currency: Vietnamese dollar.
Flag: Orange, with three horizontal crimson stripes in centre.

Western Samoa
Principal language: Samoan.
Principal religion: Protestant.
Head of State: Prince.
Currency: Samoan pound.
Flag: Five white stars on royal blue quarter next to staff. Remaining three-quarters red.

Yemen
Principal language: Arabic.
Principal religion: Islamic.
Head of State: King and President (part Royalist state, part Republican).
Currency: Yemeni riyal.
Flag: Horizontal bands of red, white, black, with green star in centre

53

of white band (adopted 1962).

Yugoslavia
Principal languages: Serbian, Croatian, Slovene, Macedonian.
Principal religions: Eastern Orthodox, Roman Catholic.
Head of State: President.
Currency: Dinar.
Flag: Three horizontal bars, blue, white, red, with red star, outlined
in yellow, in centre.

Zaire
See Congo.

Great Britain and the Commonwealth

The Royal Family
The Queen's official style is "Her Most Excellent Majesty
ELIZABETH II, by the Grace of God, of the United Kingdom of Great
Britain and Northern Ireland and of Her other Realms and Ter-
ritories Queen, Head of the Commonwealth, Defender of the Faith."
She is the elder daughter of the late King George VI and of Her
Majesty Queen Elizabeth the Queen Mother, and was born at 17
Bruton Street, London, W. 1, on April 21, 1926. Her full names are
Elizabeth Alexandra Mary. She succeeded to the Throne on
February 6, 1952, the fourth Sovereign of the Royal House of
Windsor, and was crowned at Westminster Abbey on June 2, 1953.
She married on November 20, 1947, in Westminster Abbey, Philip,
Duke of Edinburgh, Earl of Merioneth and Baron Greenwich, KG,
PC, KT, GMBE, FRS (now styled His Royal Highness Prince Philip,
Duke of Edinburgh).
They have four children. They are:

H.R.H. The Prince of Wales
Charles Philip Arthur George, Prince of Wales and Earl of Chester,
Duke of Cornwall and Duke of Rothesay, Earl of Carrick and Baron
Renfrew, Lord of the Isles and Great Steward of Scotland, KG. Born
at Buckingham Palace on November 14, 1948.

H.R.H. Princess Anne Elizabeth Alice Louise
Born at Clarence House on August 15, 1950.
She married on November 14, 1973, in Westminster Abbey, Captain
Mark Anthony Peter Phillips, CVO, of 1st Queen's Dragoon Guards.

H.R.H. Prince Andrew Albert Christian Edward
Born at Buckingham Palace on February 19, 1960.

H.R.H. Prince Edward Antony Richard Louis
Born at Buckingham Palace on March 10, 1964.

The Order of Succession to the Crown
1. H.R.H. The Prince of Wales.
2. H.R.H. Prince Andrew.
3. H.R.H. Prince Edward.
4. H.R.H. Princess Anne.
5. H.R.H. Princess Margaret Rose, CI, GCVO, Countess of Snowdon. Born at Glamis Castle, Angus, Scotland, on August 21, 1930, she is the Queen's only sister. On May 6, 1960, in Westminster Abbey, she married Antony Charles Robert Armstrong-Jones (born March 7, 1930), who was created Earl of Snowdon in 1961.
6. David Albert Charles Armstrong-Jones, Viscount Linley, son of Princess Margaret, born November 3, 1961.
7. Lady Sarah Frances Elizabeth Armstrong-Jones, daughter of Princess Margaret, born May 1, 1964.
8. H.R.H. Prince Richard Alexander Walter George, Duke of Gloucester, born August 26, 1944.

Kings of England (since A.D. 927)

*Before the year 927, England was composed of nine separate little kingdoms, Kent, South Saxons, West Saxons, Bernicia, Northumbria, Mercia, Deira, East Angles, East Saxons, King Athelstan, grandson of King Alfred of the West Saxons, was the first to establish rule over all England, which he did in 927. This overall rule was lost from time to time in succeeding years.

Name	Parents	Married	Came to throne	Length of reign	Died
Athelstan b. 895	Edward the Elder and Queen Egwyn	—	925	15 yrs.	940 age 45
Edmund b. 921	Edward the Elder and Queen Eadgifu	1. Elgifu 2. Ethelfled	940	6 yrs.	946 age 25
Edred b. 923	Edward the Elder and Queen Eadgifu	—	946	9 yrs.	955 age 32
Edwy b. 941	King Edmund and Queen Elgifu	—	955	4 yrs.	959 age 18
Edgar b. 943	King Edmund and Queen Elgifu	1. Ethelfled 2. Elfthryth	959	16 yrs.	975 age 32
Edward the Martyr b. 963	King Edgar and Queen Ethelfled	—	975	3 yrs.	978 age 17
Ethelred II (The Unready) b. 968	King Edgar and Queen Elfthryth	1. Elfgifu 2. Emma, dau. of Duke of Normandy	978	37 yrs.	1016 age 48
Edmund Ironside b. 989	King Ethelred II and Queen Elfgifu	—	1016	6 mths	1016 age 27
Canute the Dane b. 995	King Swegn Forkbeard of Denmark. Took throne by force	1. Elfgifu 2. Emma, widow of Ethelred	1017	18 yrs.	1035 age 40

Name	Parents	Married	Came to throne	Length of reign	Died
Harold I b. 1016?	King Canute and Queen Elfgifu	—	1035	5 yrs.	1040 age 24
Hardicanute b. 1018	King Canute and Queen Emma	—	1040	2 yrs.	1042 age 24
Edward The Confessor b. 1004	King Ethelred II and Queen Emma	1. Emma, dau. of Earl Godwin	1042	24 yrs.	1066 age 62
Harold II b. 1022	Earl Godwin. Brother of Queen Emma	—	1066	10 mths.	1066 age 44

The House of Normandy

Name	Parents	Married	Came to throne	Length of reign	Died
William I b.1027	Duke of Normandy. Took throne by conquest	Matilda, dau. of Count of Flanders	1066	21 yrs.	1087 age 60
William II b. 1057	King William I and Queen Matilda	Unmarried	1087	13 yrs.	1100 age 43
Henry I b. 1068	King William I and Queen Matilda	1. Matilda of Scotland 2. Adelicia	1100	35 yrs.	1135 age 67
Stephen b. 1104	Count of Blois. Grandson of King William I	Matilda, dau. of Count of Boulogne	1135	19 yrs.	1154 age 50

The House of Plantagenet

Name	Parents	Married	Came to throne	Length of reign	Died
Henry II b. 1133	Geoffrey Plantagenet. Grandson of King Henry I	Eleanor, dau. of Duke of Guienne	1154	35 yrs.	1189 age 56
Richard I b. 1157	King Henry II and Queen Eleanor	Berengaria, dau. of King of Navarre	1189	10 yrs.	1199 age 42

Name	Parents	Married	Came to throne	Length of reign	Died
John b. 1167	King Henry II and Queen Eleanor	1. Avisa, dau. of Earl of Gloucester 2. Isabella, dau. of Count of Angoulême	1199	17 yrs.	1216 age 49
Henry III b. 1207	King John and Queen Isabella	Eleanor, dau. of Count of Provence	1216	56 yrs.	1272 age 65
Edward I b. 1239	King Henry III and Queen Eleanor	1. Eleanor of Castile 2. Margaret of France	1272	35 yrs.	1307 age 68
Edward II b. 1284	King Edward I and Queen Eleanor	Isabella, dau. of Philip of France	1307	20 yrs.	1327 age 43
Edward III b. 1312	King Edward II and Queen Isabella	Philippa, dau. of Count of Holland and Hainault	1327	50 yrs.	1377 age 65
Richard II b. 1367	The Black Prince. Grandson of King Edward III	1. Anne of Bohemia 2. Isabel of France	1377	22 yrs.	Deposed 1399 Died 1400 age 33
The House of Lancaster					
Henry IV b. 1366	John of Gaunt. Grandson of King Edward III	1. Mary of Bohun 2. Joanna of Navarre	1399	13 yrs.	1413 age 47
Henry V b. 1388	King Henry IV and Lady Mary of Bohun	Katherine of France	1413	9 yrs.	1422 age 34

Name	Parents	Married	Came to throne	Length of reign	Died
Henry VI b. 1421	King Henry V and Queen Katherine	Margaret of Anjou	1422	39 yrs.	Deposed 1461 Died 1471 age 49
The House of York					
Edward IV b. 1442	Richard, Duke of York. Great-great-grandson of King Edward III	Elizabeth, dau. of Sir Richard Woodville	1461	22 yrs.	1483 age 41
Edward V b. 1470	King Edward IV and Queen Elizabeth	Unmarried	1483	About 3 mths.	1483 age 13
Richard III b. 1452	Richard, Duke of York. Brother of King Edward IV	Anne, dau. of Earl of Warwick	1483	2 yrs.	1485 age 33
The House of Tudor					
Henry VII b. 1457	Grandson of Owen Tudor and Katherine, widow of Henry V	Elizabeth, dau. of King Edward IV	1485	24 yrs.	1509 age 53
Henry VIII b. 1491	King Henry VII and Queen Elizabeth	1. Katherine of Aragon (Div.) 2. Anne Boleyn (Beheaded) 3. Jane Seymour (Died) 4. Anne of Cleves (Divorced)	1509	38 yrs.	1547 age 56

Name	Parents	Married	Came to throne	Length of reign	Died
		5. Katherine Howard (Beheaded) 6. Katherine Parr			
Edward VI b. 1537	King Henry VIII and Jane Seymour	Unmarried	1547	6 yrs.	1553 age 16
Lady Jane Grey b. 1537	Marquess of Dorset. Great-niece of Henry VIII	Lord Guildford Dudley	1553	14 days.	1554 age 17
Mary I b. 1516	King Henry VIII and Katherine of Aragon	Philip of Spain	1553	5 yrs.	1558 age 43
Elizabeth I b. 1533	King Henry VIII and Anne Boleyn	Unmarried	1558	44 yrs.	1603 age 69

The House of Stuart

Name	Parents	Married	Came to throne	Length of reign	Died
James I b. 1566	Mary, Queen of Scots. Great-great-grandson of King Henry VII	Anne of Denmark	1603	22 yrs.	1625 age 59
Charles I b. 1600	King James I and Queen Anne	Henrietta-Maria of France	1625	24 yrs.	1649 age 48
Charles II b. 1630	King Charles I and Queen Henrietta-Maria	Catherine of Braganza	1649 (Restored 1660)	36 yrs.	1685 age 55

(Note: Commonwealth declared 1649 after Charles I's execution. Oliver Cromwell, Lord Protector, 1653-1658; Richard Cromwell, Lord Protector, 1658-1659).

Name	Parents	Married	Came to throne	Length of reign	Died
James II	King Charles I and	1. Lady Anne Hyde	1685	3 yrs.	Deposed

Name	Parents	Married	Came to throne / Length of reign	Died
b. 1633	Queen Henrietta-Maria	2. Mary of Modena		1688 Died 1701 age 68
William III b. 1650 and	William of Orange		Jointly 13 yrs. 1689	1702 age 51
Mary II b. 1662	King James II and Lady Anne Hyde		6 yrs.	1694 age 33
Anne b. 1665	King James II and Lady Anne Hyde	Prince George of Denmark	1702 12 yrs.	1714 age 49

The House of Hanover

Name	Parents	Married	Came to throne / Length of reign	Died
George I b. 1660	Elector of Hanover and Sophia (grand-dau. of James I)	Sophia of Zell	1714 13 yrs.	1727 age 67
George II b. 1683	King George I and Sophia of Zell	Caroline of Brandenburg-Auspach	1727 33 yrs.	1760 age 77
George III b. 1738	Frederick, Prince of Wales. Grandson of King George II	Charlotte of Mecklenburg-Strelitz	1760 59 yrs.	1820 age 81
George IV b. 1762	King George III and Queen Charlotte	1. Mary Anne Fitzherbert 2. Caroline of Brunswick-Wolfenbüttel	1820 10 yrs.	1830 age 67

Name	Parents	Married	Came to throne	Length of reign	Died
William IV b. 1765	King George III and Queen Charlotte	Adelaide of Saxe-Meiningen	1830	7 yrs.	1837 age 71
Victoria b. 1819	Duke of Kent. Grand-daughter of George III	Albert of Saxe-Coburg and Gotha	1837	63 yrs.	1901 age 81
The House of Saxe-Coburg					
Edward VII b. 1841	Queen Victoria and Prince Albert	Princess Alexandra of Denmark	1901	9 yrs.	1910 age 68
The House of Windsor					
George V b. 1865	King Edward VII and Queen Alexandra	Princess Mary of Teck	1910	25 yrs.	1936 age 70
Edward VIII b. 1894	King George V and Queen Mary	Mrs. Wallis Simpson	1936	325 days	Abdicated 1936
George VI b. 1895	King George V and Queen Mary	The Lady Elizabeth Angela Marguerite, dau. of the 14th Earl of Strathmore and Kinghorne (H.M. Queen Elizabeth the Queen Mother)	1936	15 yrs.	1952 age 56
Elizabeth II b. 1926	King George VI and Queen Elizabeth	Philip, son of Prince Andrew of Greece. (H.R.H. the Duke of Edinburgh)	1952	—	—

The Act of Settlement

Since the Act of Settlement came into force on February 6, 1701, the succession to the Crown has been clearly laid down. The Act's main aim was to exclude Roman Catholics from the British throne. The Act stated that, failing issue from H.R.H. The Princess (later Queen) Anne, daughter of King James II, and/or from any subsequent marriage by the widower King William III, the Crown would vest in Princess Sophia, Dowager Electress of Hanover and granddaughter of King James I, and her heirs. It added the proviso that all Roman Catholics or anyone marrying a Roman Catholic were for ever to be excluded "as if they were naturally dead". Queen Elizabeth II's right of succession dates from this Act.

On December 11, 1936, however, a change in statute law came about with His Majesty's Declaration of Abdication Act, 1936, by which H.R.H. The Prince Edward, MC (later the Duke of Windsor) and any children he might subsequently have were excluded from the succession.

On succeeding to the Crown, the Sovereign must:
1. join in Communion with the established Church of England.
2. declare that he or she is a Protestant.
3. swear the oaths for the preservation of the Established Church of England and the Presbyterian Church of Scotland.
4. take the Coronation Oath, which forms the basis of the contract between Sovereign and subjects.

The Peerage

There are two forms of peerage—temporal and spiritual. The five ranks of the temporal peerage are, in order of importance: dukes, marquesses, earls, viscounts, barons. The spiritual peerage belongs to the Church and has two ranks: archbishops (Canterbury and York) and 24 of the bishops. All these are entitled to sit in the House of Lords.

Principal Orders and Decorations

Orders, Decorations and Medals are bestowed by the Sovereign, usually on the advice of Government. Anyone receiving one is entitled to put the letters of the order or decoration after his name. The order in which the letters of more than one decoration are placed is specifically laid down. The list of 62 orders, etc., in existence is given below. Those marked with an asterisk are no longer awarded.

1.	VC	Victoria Cross
2.	GC	George Cross
3.	KG	Knight of the Most Noble of the Garter
4.	KT	Knight of the Most Ancient and Most Noble Order of the Thistle
*5.	KP	Knight of the Most Illustrious Order of St. Patrick

6.	GCB	Knight Grand Cross of the Most Honourable Order of the Bath
7.	OM	Member of the Order of Merit
*8.	GCSI	Knight Grand Commander of the Most Excellent Order of the Star of India
9.	GCMG	Knight Grand Cross of the Most Distinguished Order of St. Michael and St. George
*10	GCIE	Knight Grand Commander of the Most Eminent Order of the Indian Empire
*11.	CI	Lady of the Imperial Order of the Crown of India
12.	GCVO	Knight (or Dame) Grand Cross of the Royal Victorian Order
13.	GBE	Knight (or Dame) Grand Cross of the Most Excellent Order of the British Empire
14.	CH	Member of Order of Companions of Honour
15.	KCB	Knight Commander of the Most Honourable Order of the Bath
*16.	KCSI	Knight Commander of the Most Excellent Order of the Star of India
17.	KCMG	Knight Commander of the Most Distinguished Order of St. Michael and St. George
*18.	KCIE	Knight Commander of the Most Eminent Order of the Indian Empire
19.	KCVO	Knight Commander of the Royal Victorian Order
20.	DCVO	Dame Commander of the Royal Victorian Order
21.	KBE	Knight Commander of the Most Excellent Order of the British Empire
22.	DBE	Dame Commander of the Most Excellent Order of the British Empire
23.	CB	Companion of the Most Honourable Order of the Bath
*24.	CSI	Companion of the Most Excellent Order of the Star of India
25.	CMG	Companion of the Most Distinguished Order of St. Michael and St. George
*26.	CIE	Companion of the Most Eminent Order of the Star of India
27.	CVO	Companion of the Royal Victorian Order
28.	CBE	Commander of the Most Excellent Order of the British Empire
29.	DSO	Companion of the Distinguished Service Order
30.	MVO	Member of the Royal Victorian Order
31.	OBE	Officer of the Most Excellent Order of the British Empire
32.	ISO	Companion of the Imperial Service Order

	MVO	Member of the Royal Victorian Order (if 5th class)
33.	MBE	Member of the Most Excellent Order of the British Empire
*34.	IOM	(Military) Indian Order of Merit
35.	RRC	Member of the Royal Red Cross
36.	DSC	Distinguished Service Cross
37.	MC	Military Cross
38.	DFC	Distinguished Flying Cross
39.	AFC	Air Force Cross
40.	ARRC	Associate of the Royal Red Cross
*41.	OBI	Order of British India
42.	AM	Albert Medal
43.	DCM	Distinguished Conduct Medal
44.	CGM	Conspicuous Gallantry Medal
45.	GM	George Medal
46.	EM	Edward Medal
	DCM	(If for the Royal West African Frontier Force of the King's African Rifles) Distinguished Conduct Medal
*47.	IDSM	Indian Distinguished Service Medal
48.	DSM	Distinguished Service Medal
49.	MM	Military Medal
50.	DFM	Distinguished Flying Medal
51.	AFM	Air Force Medal
52.	SGM	Sea Gallantry Medal
*	IOM	(Civil) Indian Order of Merit
53.	BEM	British Empire Medal
54.	CM	Canada Medal
55.	MSM	Medal for Meritorious Service
56.	ERD	Army Emergency Reserve Decoration
*57.	VD	Volunteer Officer's Decoration
*58.	ED	Colonial Auxiliary Forces Officers' Decoration
59.	TD	Territorial Decoration
	ED	Efficiency Decoration
60.	RD	Decoration for Officers of the Royal Naval Reserve
*61.	VRD	Decoration for Officers of the Royal Naval Volunteer Reserve
62.	CD	Canadian Forces Decoration

The Union Jack is flown from public buildings on certain days of the year. Union Jack Days are shown in the table below:

Date	Reason
Feb 6	Her Majesty's Accession (1952)
Feb 19	Prince Andrew's Birthday
Mar 1	St. David (Wales only)

Date		Reason
Mar	10	Prince Edward's Birthday
Mar	25	Annunciation
Apr	21	Her Majesty's Birthday
Apr	23	St. George (England only)
May	24	Commonwealth Day
June	2	Coronation Day
June	10	Duke of Edinburgh's Birthday
Aug	4	The Queen Mother's Birthday
Aug	15	Princess Anne's Birthday
Aug	21	Princess Margaret's Birthday
Nov	14	Prince of Wales's Birthday
Nov	20	Her Majesty's Wedding Anniversary
Nov	30	St. Andrew (Scotland only)
Dec	21	St. Thomas

Note: The Union Jack is flown on days fixed for Her Majesty's Official Birthday, on Remembrance Sunday and, in the Greater London area, on the day of the opening and closing of Parliament. Additional days may be notified by the Minister of Works.

Countries of the Commonwealth

Name	Status	Area in sq. km.	Capital	Flag
Canada	Dominion	9,976,185	Ottawa	Red maple leaf on white ground, flanked by vertical red bars.
Australia	Commonwealth	7,704,165	Canberra	Blue, with one large and five small white stars. Union Jack at upper hoist.
New Zealand	Dominion	268,676	Wellington	Blue, with four red stars, edged with white, and Union Jack at upper hoist.
India	Republic	3,046,247	New Delhi	Three horizontal bars of saffron, white and green. Dark blue Asoka wheel in centre.
Bangladesh	Republic	142,776	Dacca	Dark green, with red circle in centre.
Ceylon (Sri Lanka)	Republic	65,584	Colombo	Maroon, with gold border and pinnacle in each corner. Gold lion in centre and

Name	Status	Area in sq. km.	Capital	Flag
				two vertical stripes of green and saffron at staff.
Ghana	Republic	237,873	Accra	Horizontal bars of red, white, green. Black star in centre.
Malaysia	Federation	333,214	Kuala Lumpur	Equal horizontal stripes in red (7) and white (7). Yellow star and crescent in royal blue canton.
Singapore	Republic	585	Singapore	Two equal horizontal bands, red and white, with a white crescent and stars in the upper corner of the hoist.
Nigeria	Federal Republic	923,773	Lagos	Equal vertical bars of green, white, green.
Cyprus	Republic	9,251	Nicosia	Gold map of Cyprus above green olive branches on white ground.
Sierra Leone	Independent State	72,326	Freetown	Horizontal bars of green, white, blue.
Tanzania	Republic	942,004	Dar-es-Salaam	Black diagonal stripe dividing triangles of green and blue. Each triangle in turn divided by yellow stripe.
Jamaica	Independent State	10,961	Kingston	Diagonal gold cross on black and green.
Trinidad and Tobago	Independent State	5,128	Port-of-Spain	Red, divided by white-edged black diagonal stripe.
Uganda	Republic	239,640	Kampala	Six bars of black, gold, red. Uganda crane on white disc.
Kenya	Republic	582,646	Nairobi	Horizontal bars of black, red, green, separated by white stripes. Shield is superimposed.
Malawi	Independent	118,485	Zomba	Horizontal stripes of

Name	Status	Area in sq. km.	Capital	Flag
	dent State			black, red, green.
Malta	Independent State	316	Valletta	White and red vertical halves, with George Cross on blue canton.
Zambia	Republic	752,618	Lusaka	Blue shield bearing yellow eagle holding a white fish. Below, seven black and six white wavy "pallets".
Gambia	Republic	10,360	Bathurst	Brown elephant, palm tree and green mountains on yellow. Red letter, G, below.
Bahamas	Colony	11,406	Nassau	(Badge): Royal crown and three sailing ships on shield.
Bermuda	Colony	54	Hamilton	(Badge): Red lion supporting a shield and seated on a green mound.
Botswana (formerly Basutoland)	Independent State	30,344	Maseru	(Badge): Crocodile between two sheaths in gold on olive green shield.
British Honduras	Colony	22,965	Belize	(Badge): Shield with Union Jack, axes and saw and a sailing ship at sea.
British Indian Ocean Territory	Colony	—	Islands	—
British Solomon Islands	Protectorate	29,785	Honiara	(Badge): Shield with gold lion, eagle, turtle, bow, four spears, Melanesian dancing shield, two frigate birds.
British Virgin Islands	Colony	153	Road Town	(Badge): Wise virgin and 12 gold lamps on green shield.
Brunei	Protectorate	5,765	Brunei Town	Two diagonal bands, white and black, on

Name	Status	Area in sq. km.	Capital	Flag
				a yellow ground.
Falkland Islands	Colony	16,265	Port Stanley	(Badge): White circle with blue shield and gold ship on white wavy bars.
Fiji	Colony	18,234	City of Suva	(Badge): Shield with gold lion holding cocoa pod; three sugar canes, coconut palm, dove and bananas in St. George's Cross.
Gibraltar		6.5	—	(Badge): Triple-towered castle with golden key on a red shield.
Gilbert and Ellice Islands	Colony	956	—	(Badge): Gold frigate bird on red sky; gold sun rising from blue and white wavy sea.
Guyana (formerly British Guiana)	Independent State	214,970	George-town	(Badge): White circle containing a shield bearing a three-masted sailing ship on a green sea.
Hong Kong	Colony	1,031	Victoria	(Badge): Two Chinese junks, surmounted by a naval crown.
Lesotho (formerly Bechuanaland)	Independent State	574,980	Mafeking	Blue field, with white Basuto hat in centre, and red and green stripes next to the hoist.
Mauritius	Independent State	2,095	Port Louis	(Badge): Arms showing gold galley, three palm trees, red key, white star.
New Hebrides	Anglo-French Condominium	14,763	Vila	(Badge): Royal crown on white disc.
Pitcairn	Colony	5.2	Adams-town	—

Name	Status	Area in sq. km.	Capital	Flag
St. Helena Ascension Tristan da Cunha (islands)	Colony	122 88 98	James-town	(Badge): Yellow scroll, showing ship flying the cross of St. George, sailing between two cliffs.
Seychelles (islands)	Colony	404	Port Victoria	(Badge): Palm tree with turtle and three distant palm trees.
Swaziland	Protec-torate	17,363	Mbabane	Red, with horizontal blue stripes at top and bottom divided from the red by thin gold stripes. In the centre is a native shield and weapons
Tonga	Kingdom under U.K. protection	699	Nuku'al-ofa	Red, with truncated red cross on white canton.
West Indies				
Antigua	Associated State	443	St. John's	—
Barbados	Indepen-dent State	430	Bridgetown	—
Cayman Is.	Colony	259	Georgetown	—
Mont-serrat	Colony	84	Plymouth	—
St. Kitts-Nevis-Anguilla	Associated State	357	Basseterre	—
Turks and Caicos Is.	Colony	430	Grand Turk Island	—
Windward Islands				
Grenada	Associated State	344	St. George's	—

Name	Status	Area in sq. km.	Capital	Flag
St. Lucia	Colony	616	Castries	—
St. Vincent	Colony	388	Kingstown	—
Dominica	Associated State	751	Roseau	—

Note: The British Antarctic Territory covers an area of about 5,698,000 square km. and includes the South Shetland Islands, the South Orkney Islands and part of the mainland of Antarctica. It is classed as a Crown Colony although it has no permanent inhabitants. Southern Rhodesia is not included in the above list because its Prime Minister, Mr Ian Smith, made a Unilateral Declaration of Independence at the end of 1965, an illegal action. Although Mr Smith reaffirmed his country's allegiance to the Queen, his administration is regarded as a rebel government by the British. Previously, Southern Rhodesia had been a self-governing colony. Its capital is Salisbury and it covers an area of 389,362 square km.

Great Britain—Part 2

The British Constitution

The British Constitution is the basis of our form of government and, consequently, our whole way of life. Yet there is no document that lays down the rules of the Constitution—unlike the Constitutions of most other countries—and this gives it a valuable flexibility. The Constitution has grown up over the centuries and it is now universally accepted as the world's most workable form of government.

Parliament—the governing body of the country—has been in existence for 700 years. The first Parliament was summoned by

Houses of Parliament

Simon de Montfort in 1265. In the name of the King, he called to Parliament not only the great men of the land, the prelates, earls and barons, but also two elected representatives from every county, city and town. Today, there are two Houses of Parliament, the House of Lords and the House of Commons.

The House of Lords is composed of about 900 Lords Spiritual and Temporal. The Lords Spiritual are the Archbishops of Canterbury and York, the Bishops of London, Durham and Winchester and 21 other senior Bishops. The Lords Temporal are the peers and peeresses by descent of England, Scotland, Great Britain or the United Kingdom, new peers, Lords of Appeal in Ordinary (who are life peers) and Life Peers and Life Peeresses created under the Life Peerages Act 1958. Under the Peerage Act 1963, a person inheriting a peerage may within one year (or one month in the case of a Member of the House of Commons) disclaim the peerage for life. The right of his heirs to the peerage is not affected.

The House of Commons has a total membership of 630, each member representing one of the 630 parliamentary constituencies of Great Britain. He is elected by the votes of the people.

The Sovereign, as Head of State, has a great number of theoretical powers. He or she makes peace and war, issues charters, creates peers, appoints the Prime Minister, summons or dissolves Parliament, gives the Royal Assent to laws passed by Parliament. In practice, the Sovereign would be unlikely to act against the advice of his or her ministers. In a sense, this makes the Monarch little more than a puppet figure but, because he or she is considered to be "above politics", and cannot in fairness be blamed for the actions of the Government, the Royal Family is probably more highly regarded and held in greater affection by the British people today than at any other time in Britain's history.

Legislation

Any ordered community must have laws by which its people may live in peace. Your school has laws—though they are probably called rules—which apply to every member of the school. They were drawn up by your teachers and you know the penalties for breaking them. Similarly, Great Britain, which is a community of more than 50,000,000 people, has laws and these were formed by Parliament. A new law starts life as a *Bill* and can be introduced either by the Government of the day or by a private Member of Parliament. A Bill, except a Money Bill which must originate in the House of Commons, can be introduced in either House, when it receives its *First Reading*. The next stage is the *Second Reading* when it is debated by the House. If passed, it is referred to a Committee (that is, a Committee of the whole House, a Select Committee, appointed for a specific purpose, or a Standing Committee, which considers public bills). This is called the *Committee Stage*, and the Bill is discussed clause by clause before being returned to the House with or without amendment. The next step is the *Report Stage*, when it is either accepted or referred back to the same or another Committee. Finally, the Bill receives its *Third Reading* and is sent to the other House. Once a Bill has been passed by both Houses, it becomes an *Act of Parliament*, provided the Sovereign has given it the *Royal Assent*. The Sovereign is allowed to withhold assent (sometimes called the *Royal Veto*) but this has not happened since 1707 in the reign of Queen Anne.

Political Parties

Most Members of Parliament belong to a political party, whose collective views they normally share. Before a General Election, each party prepares the plans it will carry out should it be given an overall majority by the electorate and thus be able to form a government. These plans are published in what is called a *Manifesto*. Today, most Members of the House of Commons represent a particular party, so that, although the voters may not know a candidate personally, their decision to vote for him depends on whether they like the party he belongs to. Once elected, a Member is expected to follow his party's policies and to vote in the House of Commons according to the party line. This can be very important where a Government has only a small majority because a defeat if the Government in a vital debate means that the party in power can no longer govern efficiently and the Prime Minister may decide to dissolve Parliament and hold a General Election.

The vote taken at the end of the Parliamentary debate is known as a *Division*. To ensure that its members are present in the House for an important division, each party appoints a few of its members to act as *Whips*. The Whips keep members informed of forthcoming debates—usually by means of a circular letter or appeal, which is also known as a "whip". For a particularly important debate, the letter will be underlined three times and headed "Most Important". Failure by the Member to respond to a three-line whip could mean that his party's support is withdrawn from him. He would, of course, still remain a Member of Parliament, but his future career within the party could be jeopardised. And at the next election, he could find that he no longer had the financial support of the party.

The main political parties in Britain today are the *Labour Party,* the *Conservative Party* and the *Liberal Party.* The Conservatives and the Liberals are the two oldest parties, dating back to the reign of King Charles II, when they were known respectively as the Tories and the Whigs. The term Tory is still used for the Conservative Party, although the Liberals are never nowadays called Whigs. The Labour Party, or Socialists as they are often called, came into being in the 1890s. The Liberal Party has declined in importance during the past 40 years or so, a decline which has been matched by the rise of the Labour Party. There are several smaller parties, which often put up candidates at an election, such as the *Communist Party,* the *Welsh Nationalist Party,* the *Scottish Nationalist Party,* and the *Irish Social and Democratic Labour Party.*

Election deposits

When a person is nominated as a candidate, he must pay £150 deposit to the *Returning Officer,* the man responsible for organising elections in a constituency. The money is returnable only if the candidate receives more than one-eighth of the total vote.

The Prime Minister

After an election is over and all the votes have been counted, the leader of the party which has gained the largest number of seats is summoned by the Sovereign and invited to form a Government. The position of Prime Minister has been in existence since 1721. although it was not officially recognised until 1905. The Prime Minister's chief constitutional duty is to act as a link between the Administration and the Crown. He sends all important State documents and correspondence to the Sovereign and advises him or her when to dissolve Parliament. Since 1721, the office has been held by the following:

Name	Government	Took office
Sir Robert Walpole	Whig	Apr 3, 1721
Earl of Wilmington	Whig	Feb 16, 1742
Henry Pelham	Whig	Aug 25, 1743
Duke of Newcastle	Whig	May 18, 1754
Duke of Devonshire	Whig	Nov 16, 1756
Duke of Newcastle	Whig	July 2, 1757
Earl of Bute	Tory	May 28, 1762
George Grenville	Whig	Apr 15, 1763
Marquess of Rockingham	Whig	July 10, 1765
Earl of Chatham	Whig	Aug 2, 1766
Duke of Grafton	Whig	Dec —, 1767
Lord North	Tory	Feb 6, 1770
Marquess of Rockingham	Whig	Mar 27, 1782
Earl of Shelburne	Whig	July 13, 1782
Duke of Portland	Coalition	Apr 4, 1783
William Pitt	Tory	Dec 7, 1783
Henry Addington	Tory	Mar 21, 1801
William Pitt	Tory	May 16, 1804
Lord Grenville	Whig	Feb 10, 1806
Duke of Portland	Tory	Mar 31, 1807
Spencer Perceval	Tory	Dec 6, 1809
Earl of Liverpool	Tory	June 16, 1812
George Canning	Tory	Apr 30, 1827
Viscount Goderich	Tory	Sept 8, 1827
Duke of Wellington	Tory	Jan 26, 1828
Earl Grey	Whig	Nov 24, 1830
Viscount Melbourne	Whig	July 18, 1834
Sir Robert Peel	Tory	Dec 26, 1834
Viscount Melbourne	Whig	Mar 14, 1835
Sir Robert Peel	Tory	Sept 6, 1841
Lord John Russell	Whig	July 6, 1846
Earl of Derby	Tory	Feb 28, 1852
Earl of Aberdeen	Peelite	Dec 28, 1852
Viscount Palmerston	Liberal	Feb 10, 1855
Earl of Derby	Conservative	Feb 25, 1858
Viscount Palmerston	Liberal	June 18, 1858
Earl Russell	Liberal	Nov 6, 1865
Earl of Derby	Conservative	July 6, 1866
Benjamin Disraeli	Conservative	Feb 27, 1868
W. E. Gladstone	Liberal	Dec 9, 1868
Benjamin Disraeli	Conservative	Feb 21, 1874
W. E. Gladstone	Liberal	Apr 28, 1880
Marquess of Salisbury	Conservative	June 24, 1885
W. E. Gladstone	Liberal	Feb 6, 1886
Marquess of Salisbury	Conservative	Aug 3, 1886
W. E. Gladstone	Liberal	Aug 18, 1892
Earl of Rosebery	Liberal	Mar 3, 1894

Name	Government	Took office
Marquess of Salisbury	Conservative	July 2, 1895
A. J. Balfour	Conservative	July 12, 1902
Sir H. Campbell-Bannerman	Liberal	Dec 5, 1905
H. H. Asquith	Liberal	Apr 8, 1908
H. H. Asquith	Coalition	May 26, 1915
D. Lloyd George	Coalition	Dec 7, 1916
A. Bonar Law	Conservative	Oct 23, 1922
S. Baldwin	Conservative	May 22, 1923
J. R. MacDonald	Labour	Jan 22, 1924
S. Baldwin	Conservative	Nov 4, 1924
J. R. MacDonald	Labour	June 8, 1929
J. R. MacDonald	Coalition	Aug 25, 1931
S. Baldwin	Coalition	June 7, 1935
N. Chamberlain	Coalition	May 28, 1937
Winston Churchill	Coalition	May 11, 1940
Winston Churchill	Conservative	May 23, 1945
C. R. Attlee	Labour	July 26, 1945
Sir Winston Churchill	Conservative	Oct 26, 1951
Sir Anthony Eden	Conservative	Apr 6, 1955
Harold Macmillan	Conservative	Jan 13, 1957
Sir Alec Douglas-Home	Conservative	Oct 19, 1963
Harold Wilson	Labour	Oct 16, 1964
Edward Heath	Conservative	June 24, 1970
Harold Wilson	Labour	Mar 4, 1974
James Callaghan	Labour	Apr 5, 1976

Great Officers of State

The Lord High Steward. Appointed for special occasions like the Coronation.

The Lord High Chancellor (usually known simply as The Lord Chancellor). He is head of the Judiciary and appoints all Judges, except the Lord Chief Justice and the Master of the Rolls, and all Justices of the Peace. He is Speaker of the House of Lords and sits on the Woolsack. He is always a member of the Cabinet and has custody of the Great Seal.

The Lord High Treasurer.

The Lord President of the Council.

The Lord Privy Seal.

The Lord Great Chamberlain.

The Lord High Constable. Appointed for special occasions like the Coronation.

The Earl Marshal.

The Lord High Admiral. This office is held by the Queen.

Other Important Officers

First Lord of the Treasury. This position is always held by the Prime Minister.

The Speaker of the House of Commons. He is elected by the House at the start of each Parliament. He acts as spokesman and president of the Chamber and has great authority, being responsible for keeping order in the House. Although he is elected as a Member of Parliament and belongs to a political party, he is entirely neutral as Speaker and does not speak in debates nor vote in divisions.

The Palace of Westminster

Since about 1340, Parliament has been held at the royal palace of Westminster. The original palace was built by Edward the Confessor, enlarged by William the Conqueror and Westminster Hall added by William II. In 1834, the whole palace, except for Westminster Hall, was destroyed by fire. The present Houses of Parliament, designed by Sir Charles Barry and Augustus Pugin, were built on the site between the years 1840 and 1867. The Chamber of the Houses of Commons was destroyed by bombing in 1941, and the new Chamber was used for the first time in October, 1950. When Parliament is sitting, a Union Jack is flown on the Victoria Tower of the House of Lords from sunrise to sunset. The clock tower of the House of Commons displays a light from sunrise to sunset while the House is in session.

Prime Minister's Official Residences

The Prime Minister's town residence is at No. 10 Downing Street. The Chancellor of the Exchequer lives next door at No. 11, while No. 12 is the office of the Government Whips. Downing Street was named after Sir George Downing, Bt., who was M.P. for Morpeth from 1660 to 1684. The Prime Minister also has an official country residence in the Chilterns. The house is called Chequers and is a Tudor mansion, presented by Lord and Lady Lee of Fareham in 1917. The house has been used by Prime Ministers since 1921, when Lord Lee added the Chequers estate of 283 hectares.

Local Government in Great Britain
England and Wales

Local administration is carried out by four different types of bodies: (i) local branches of some central ministries, such as the Ministry of Social Security; (ii) local sub-managements of nationalised industries (coal, electricity, gas, public transport and the Post Office); (iii) specialist authorities such as the police and water conservation; and (iv) the system of *local government*. The Local Government Act of 1972 created a new system which took effect from April, 1974.

England and Wales have somewhat different systems. Each country has 3 types of council in common, i.e. *county, district* and English *parish* or Welsh *community* councils. In addition, England has some *metropolitan* county and district councils. Councillors are elected by their local electors for 4 years. A district may be granted the honorific status of a "Borough" and a parish or community council may call itself a "Town" Council. The president of a borough council is called the Mayor, or in a few famous places, the Lord Mayor. The others are called chairmen. They are elected annually by their councils.

There are 46 non-metropolitan counties (8 are in Wales) and 6 metropolitan counties. Within the counties there are 347 districts (36 metropolitan, and 311 non-metropolitan, of which 37 are in Wales).

The English districts consist of about 10,000 parishes and some 500 areas which are not parishes. About 7,000 of the parishes have councils. The Welsh districts are divided into about 1,000 communities, some 800 of which have councils.

County boundaries were laid down by the Local Government Act, 1972, and the district boundaries were settled by orders made in 1973 under that Act.

Local government functions may be classified into county, district and sub-district functions. For example, *county functions* include the formulation of development plans, traffic, transportation and roads, education, public libraries and museums, youth employment and social services.

Greater London
Since 1965, the Metropolitan area, with a population of 7.42 million has had a Greater London Council (GLC) and has been divided into 32 London Boroughs. The City is in most respects independent of the surrounding system, and has an ancient constitution.

Great Britain—Part Three

England, Non-Metropolitan Counties

Name	Population	Area in hectares	Admin. Offices
Avon	909,000	133,956	Bristol

Name	Population	Area in hectares	Admin. Offices
Bedfordshire	463,000	123,444	Bedford
Berkshire	657,600	124,314	Reading
Buckinghamshire	497,000	187,781	Aylesbury
Cambridgeshire	519,830	33,356	Cambridge
Cheshire	880,941	232,231	Chester
Cleveland	572,400	17,785	Middlesbrough
Cornwall	383,390	354,636	Truro
Cumbria	474,750	680,802	Carlisle
Derbyshire	893,600	263,092	Matlock
Devon	459,280	652,507	Exeter
Dorset	561,663	230,441	Dorchester
Durham	610,650	243,620	Durham
East Sussex	660,720	179,536	Lewes
Essex	1,386,290	367,406	Chelmsford
Gloucestershire	571,070	311,739	Gloucester
Hampshire	1,438,000	386,488	Winchester
Hereford & Worcester	595,000	392,559	Worcester
Hertfordshire	940,630	163,424	Hertford
Humberside	841,610	351,192	Kingston-upon-Hull
Isle of Wight	109,284	38,101	Newport, I.W.
Kent	1,426,410	372,998	Maidstone
Lancashire	1,350,480	300,465	Preston
Leicestershire	809,890	255,305	Leicester
Lincolnshire	512,000	588,544	Lincoln
Norfolk	625,700	956,266	Norwich
Northamptonshire	478,000	236,753	Northampton
North Yorkshire	655,000	831,658	Northallerton
Nottinghamshire	682,570	210,831	Nottingham
Oxfordshire	521,480	261,158	Oxford
Salop	345,860	349,048	Shrewsbury
Somerset	395,000	345,795	Taunton
Staffordshire	751,640	265,969	Barnsley
Suffolk	564,000	380,742	Ipswich
Surrey	995,930	165,465	Kingston-upon-Thames
Warwickshire	344,500	198,020	Warwick
West Sussex	636,500	201,670	Chichester
Wiltshire	495,280	348,082	Trowbridge

Metropolitan Counties, England

Name	Population	Area in hectares	Admin. Offices
Greater Manchester	2,770,000	128,430	Manchester
Merseyside	1,636,938	64,752	Liverpool
South Yorkshire	1,320,019	156,117	Barnsley
Tyne & Wear	1,209,000	—	Sunderland

Name	Population	Area in hectares	Admin. Offices
West Midlands	2,790,000	—	Birmingham
West Yorkshire	2,077,896	203,913	Wakefield

Wales

In Wales, Glamorgan is divided into three counties and the other five new counties are formed as a result of mergers among the remaining twelve.

Name	Population	Area in hectares	Admin. Offices
Clwyd	371,000	242,415	Mold
Dyfed	315,000	576,697	Carmarthen
Gwent	440,479	137,742	Newport, Monmouthshire
Gwynedd	224,354	386,488	Caernarvon
Mid Glamorgan	533,310	101,876	Cardiff
Powys	99,000	507,898	Llandrindod Wells
South Glamorgan	389,916	41,606	Cardiff
West Glamorgan	371,867	81,537	Swansea

Scotland

Radical changes in Scottish local government were set forth in a parliamentary bill in 1972. The Local Government (Scotland) Act, 1973, came into force in May, 1975. The existing counties were abolished and eight Regional Authorities established.

Highlands Region   *approx. population 197,000*

District Councils:	Caithness	Lochaber
	Sutherland	Inverness
	Ross	Badenoch
	Lewis	Nairn
	Uist	
	Skye	

North-East Region   *approx. population 437,000*

District Councils:	Moray
	Banff-Buchanan
	Donside
	Aberdeen
	Kincardine-Deeside

East Region   *approx. population 452,000*

District Councils:	Angus

	Dundee	
	Perth and Kinross	
	North Fife	

South-East Region   *approx. population 997,000*

District Councils:	Kirkcaldy
	Dunfermline
	West Lothian
	Edinburgh
	Midlothian
	East Lothian

Borders Region   *approx. population 96,000*

District Councils:	Peebles
	Selkirk
	Roxburgh
	Berwick

Central Region   *approx. population 264,000*

District Councils:	Clackmannan
	Falkirk-Grangemouth
	Stirling

West Region   *approx. population 2,562,000*

District Councils:	Argyll	East Kilbride
	Dunbarton	Lanark
	Glasgow	Paisley
	Kirkintilloch-	Greenock-Cowal-
	Cumbernauld	Bute
	Coatbridge-	
	Airdrie	North Ayrshire
	Motherwell	South Ayrshire

South-West Region   *approx. population 156,000*

District Councils:	Wigtown-Girvan
	Kirkcudbright
	Dumfries
	East Dumfriesshire

Orkney   *approx. population 17,000*
Shetland   *approx. population 17,000*

Northern Ireland
On October 1, 1973, the County Councils were replaced by 26 District Councils.

Name	Population	Area in hectares	Admin. Offices
Antrim	33,998	56,253	Antrim
Ards Borough	50,200	36,132	Newtownards
Armagh	47,400	67,461	Armagh
Ballymena (Borough)	51,000	653	Ballymena
Ballymoney	22,600	41,785	Ballymoney
Banbridge	30,300	44,530	Banbridge
Belfast City	403,900	11,516	Belfast
Carrickfergus	25,000	7,696	Carrickfergus, Co. Antrim
Castlereagh	66,700	8,445	Belfast
Coleraine	–	–	–
Cookstown (Co. Tyrone)	–	–	–
Craigavon	70,000	38,821	Portadown, Craigavon
Down	49,000	65,427	Downpatrick
Dungannon	45,224	33,517	Dungannon
Fermanagh	49,960	185,100	Enniskillen
Larne Borough	30,200	33,988	Larne
Limavady	26,000	62,162	Limavady
Lisburn Borough	70,694	44,377	Hillsbrough, Co. Down
Londonderry City	84,000	38,346	Londonderry
Magherafelt	33,000	63,538	Magherafelt, Co. Londonderry
Moyle	13,979	–	Ballycastle, Co. Antrim
Newry & Mourne	72,800	90,957	Newry
Newtownabbey	70,700	13,005	Newtownabbey, Co. Antrim
North Down	53,600	7,679	Bangor
Omagh	38,600	112,498	Omagh
Strabane	34,900	86,156	Strabane

Largest Cities

Name	Population	Name	Population
Greater London	7,353,810	Sheffield	519,703
Birmingham	1,006,760	Leeds	498,790
Glasgow	897,848	Edinburgh	449,632
Liverpool	589,000	Bristol	425,203
Manchester	531,270	Belfast	383,600

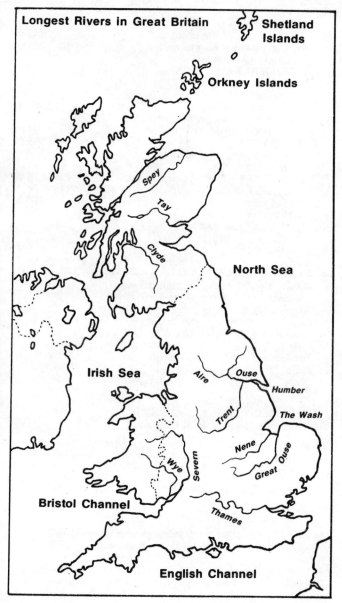

Longest Rivers in Great Britain

Shetland Islands

Orkney Islands

Spey

Tay

Clyde

North Sea

Irish Sea

Aire

Ouse

Humber

The Wash

Trent

Nene

Great Ouse

Wye

Severn

Bristol Channel

Thames

English Channel

Highest Peaks

Scotland

Ben Nevis, Inverness-shire	1,343 m.
Ben Macdhui, Aberdeenshire	1,309 m.
Braeriach, Aberdeenshire	1,295 m.
Cairn Toul, Aberdeenshire	1,293 m.
Cairngorm, Banffshire	1,245 m.

Wales

Snowdon, Gwynedd	1,085 m.
Carnedd Llewellyn, Gwynedd	1,062 m.
Carnedd Dafydd, Gwynedd	1,044 m.
Glyder Fawr, Gwynedd	999 m.
Glyder Fâch, Gwynedd	994 m.

England

Scafell Pike, Cumbria	978 m.
Sca Fell, Cumbria	964 m.
Hellvellyn, Cumbria	950 m.
Skiddaw, Cumbria	930 m.
Bow Fell, Cumbria	902 m.

Longest Rivers

Name	Mouth	Length (km.)
Severn	Bristol Channel	354
Thames	North Sea	338
Trent-Humber	North Sea	298
Aire-Ouse-Humber	North Sea	259
Ouse	The Wash	230
Wye	River Severn	217
Tay-Tummel	North Sea	188
Nene	The Wash	161
Clyde	Atlantic Ocean	158.5
Spey	North Sea	157.7

Universities in Great Britain: England

Name (No. of students)	Location	Founded
University of Oxford (11,145)	Oxford	1264 (University College)
University of Cambridge (10,832)	Cambridge	1284 (Peterhouse College)
University of Durham (3,648)	Durham	1832
University of London (37,626)	London	1836
University of Manchester (13,395)	Manchester	1851
University of Newcastle (6,017)	Newcastle-upon-Tyne	1852
University of Birmingham (7,356)	Birmingham	1900
University of Liverpool (7,800)	Liverpool	1903

Name (No. of students)	Location	Founded
University of Leeds (10,158)	Leeds	1904
University of Sheffield (6,148)	Sheffield	1905
University of Bristol (5,510)	Bristol	1909
University of Reading (5,135)	Reading	1926
University of Nottingham (5,604)	Nottingham	1938
University of Southampton (4,609)	Southampton	1952
University of Hull (3,882)	Hull	1954
University of Exeter (3,577)	Exeter	1955
University of Leicester (3,700)	Leicester	1957
University of Sussex (3,663)	Brighton	1961
University of Keele (2,364)	Keele	1962
University of East Anglia (3,113)	Norwich	1963
University of York (2,800)	York	1963
University of Lancaster (3,000)	Lancaster	1964
University of Essex (2,016)	Colchester	1964
University of Warwick (2,725)	Warwick	1965
University of Kent at Canterbury (2,900)	Canterbury	1965
Loughborough University of Technology (3,157)	Loughborough	1966
University of Aston in Birmingham (2,909)	Birmingham	1966
City University (2,400)	London	1966
Brunel University (3,113)	Uxbridge	1966
Bath University of Technology (2,815)	Bath	1966
University of Bradford (4,147)	Bradford	1966
University of Surrey (2,775)	Guildford	1966
University of Salford (3,626)	Salford	1967
The Open University (38,000)	Milton Keynes	1969

Wales

University of Wales (11,492)	Aberystwyth, Bangor, Cardiff, Swansea	1893

Scotland

University of St. Andrews (3,078)	St. Andrews, Dundee	1411
University of Glasgow (8,466)	Glasgow	1451
University of Aberdeen (5,735)	Aberdeen	1494
University of Edinburgh (11,094)	Edinburgh	1582
University of Strathclyde (6,885)	Glasgow	1965
Heriot-Watt University (2,568)	Edinburgh	1966
University of Dundee (2,796)	Dundee	1967
University of Stirling (1,940)	Stirling	1967

Northern Ireland

Queen's University of Belfast (6,626)	Belfast, Londonderry	1908
New University of Ulster (1,650)	Coleraine, Co. Londonderry	1965

The Cinque Ports

Though the word, "Cinque", comes from the French and means five, it is pronounced "sink". Originally, there were five of these ports, part of the Anglo-Saxon system (inherited from the Romans) of coastal defence between the Wash and Spithead. The five original Cinque Ports are Hastings, New Romney, Hythe, Dover and Sandwich. Some time after the Norman Conquest, two further ports were added to the group—Winchelsea and Rye. Lydd, Faversham, Folkestone, Deal, Tenterden, Margate and Ramsgate also belong to the Confederation of Cinque Ports and are known as Limbs. The present Lord Warden of the Cinque Ports is the Rt. Hon. Sir Robert Menzies, who succeeded Sir Winston Churchill in 1965.

Highway Code

Anyone taking a driving test will be examined on his knowledge of the Highway Code. Pedestrians, cyclists and riders of horses do not have to pass a test in order to use a road, but it is just as important for them to study the Highway Code and remember the rules it lays down.

Pedestrians

1. Where there is a pavement or footpath, use it.
2. Do not walk next to the kerb with your back to the oncoming traffic. Look first before stepping off the pavement.
3. Where there is no footpath, walk on the right-hand side of the road to face oncoming traffic.
4. Do not linger in the roadway or walk along cycle tracks.
5. Use subways, footbridges, pedestrian crossings or centre islands when crossing the road.
6. You have right of way on a zebra crossing, but always allow oncoming vehicles plenty of time to stop, especially when the road is wet or icy. Do not stand at a zebra crossing if you do not intend to cross. Where a zebra crossing has a centre island, each half should be treated as a separate crossing.
7. If traffic lights have "CROSS NOW" signal, do not cross until the signal appears.
8. Do not cross the road against a signal to stop by a policeman controlling the traffic.
9. Do not get off a bus except at the recognised bus-stops.

Pedal cyclists
1. If there is a special cycle track, use it.
2. In company, never ride more than two abreast. If the traffic in the road is heavy, ride in single file.
3. Never carry anything that may interfere with your control of the bicycle.
4. Do not hold on to a moving vehicle or another cyclist.
5. Do not ride close behind a moving vehicle.

By law, you must:
1. See that your cycle has efficient brakes.
2. Observe traffic signs and signals and the directions of a policeman controlling traffic.
3. Stop when signalled to do so by a School Crossing Patrol.
4. Stop for pedestrians waiting to cross the road by a zebra crossing.
5. Stop for pedestrians at a panda crossing when the flashing amber light is showing.
6. See that, at night, your front and rear lamps are alight and that your cycle has an efficient red reflector.
7. Keep to the nearside edge of the road when wheeling your cycle along the road at night without lights.
8. Stop when asked to do so by a policeman in uniform.

Riders and those in charge of animals
1. Do not let your dog stray. When taking it for a walk, keep it under close control.
2. Make sure that the road is clear before allowing or taking animals on to the road.
3. If you are riding a horse, keep to the left.
4. When leading an animal along the road, always place yourself between it and the traffic.
5. If you are herding animals along the road and there is someone

I am turning left

I am turning right

Stop	**Come on**

*To vehicle approaching
from front*

*To vehicle approaching
from front*

*To vehicle approaching
from behind*

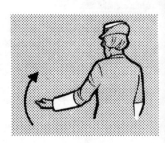

*To vehicle approaching
from behind*

*To vehicles approaching
from both front and behind*

*To vehicles approaching
from both front and behind*

with you, send him on ahead to warn traffic at danger points, such as bends and the brows of hills. Always carry lights after sunset.

Police Signals
The sketches on page 88 show the signals given by policemen on point-duty.

Traffic Signs
Throughout the country, the old traffic signs are gradually being replaced by new ones which are similar to those used on the Continent. Some of the more important ones are shown below. It is important to remember them, especially if you ride a bicycle out in the road.

Signs Giving Orders

Stop and give way

Give way to traffic on major road

Turn left ahead (right if symbol reversed)

Turn left (right if symbol reversed)

Ahead only

Plate supplementing "Turn" signs

Keep left (right if symbol reversed)

Pass either side

No entry

No right turn

No left turn

School crossing ahead

Red

Blue

Yellow

Black

No cycling or moped-riding

Route for cyclists and moped riders (compulsory)

All vehicles prohibited

Warning Signs

Steep hill downwards

Steep hill upwards

Pedestrian crossing

Road works

Slippery road

Accident

Danger: plate indicates nature of danger

Level crossing without barrier ahead

Uneven road

Cyclists and moped riders only

Information Signs

90

Traffic Light Signals
Accidents can be caused by a misunderstanding of traffic lights. Study the drawings and remember the instructions.

Red means stop. Wait behind the stop-line on the roadway.

Red and **Amber** together also mean stop. Do not go on until the green light shows.

Green means you may go on IF the road is clear. If you are turning left or right, give way to pedestrians who are crossing.

 RED

 AMBER

 GREEN

Amber alone means stop at the stop-line. You may only go on if you have passed the stop-line when the light appears.

Green Arrow means that you may go in the direction shown by the arrow, whatever other lights may be showing.

The English Language

Parts of Speech
There are eight parts of speech, dependent on how a word is used in a sentence. They are:

Nouns—denoting persons or things. Proper nouns, such as the names of people or cities, take capital letters.

Adjectives—words used to describe nouns (colour, size, etc.).

Pronouns—these are used in place of nouns or adjectives and are divided into categories (personal, I or we; demonstrative, there or that; interrogative, where or whose; indefinite, one; distributive, each or either; reflexive, himself, themselves).

Verbs—words of action or state. Thus, to behave or to feel. Transitive verbs take an object, intransitive verbs do not. A transitive verb can be used in both the active and the passive, while an intransitive verb can only be used in the active. For example: I clean the car (active); The car was cleaned by me (passive). The verb, to clean, is transitive. The sentence, I laugh loudly, however, uses the intransitive verb, to laugh. The word, loudly, is an adverb.

Adverbs—words which describe either verbs or adjectives. They usually have the suffix, -ly.

Prepositions—words which denote relationship between words or phrases. For example, to, for, under.

Conjunctions—these connect words, phrases or sentences. And, but, although are good examples.

Interjections—words or phrases that stand outside the form of a sentence. They express emotion—Goodness me! Help! Hurrah! Oh!

Foreign phrases
The English language is sprinkled with words and phrases that have been borrowed from abroad. People use them because their meaning is more exact than their English translation. The following list gives the most widely used:

Term	Language	English meaning
ab origine	Latin	from the beginning
ad astra	Latin	to the stars
ad extremum	Latin	to the last
ad hoc	Latin	for this purpose
ad idem	Latin	to the same point
ad infinitum	Latin	to infinity
ad nauseam	Latin	to a sickening degree
ad valorem	Latin	according to value
aide-de-camp	French	assistant
aide mémoire	French	aid to memory

Term	Language	English meaning
à la carte	French	dishes on the menu apart from the set meal
à la mode	French	in fashion
al fresco	Italian	in the open air
alma mater	Latin	one's old school (literally, benign mother)
amour-propre	French	self-esteem
anno Domini	Latin	in the year of our Lord
ante	Latin	before
ante meridiem	Latin	before noon
au contraire	French	on the contrary
au courant	French	fully acquainted with
au fait	French	conversant with
au fond	French	fundamentally
au naturel	French	plain, in a natural state
au pair	French	on mutual terms
au revoir	French	till we meet again
auf wiedersehen	German	till we meet again
bon marché	French	bargain, cheap
bona fide	Latin	genuine
cachet	French	distinguishing mark, characteristic
carte blanche	French	permission to do as one wishes
casus belli	Latin	justification for war
cause célèbre	French	famous lawsuit
chacun à son goût	French	each to his own taste
ci-devant	French	former
circa	Latin	about, around
cognoscente	Italian	connoisseur
comme ci, comme ça	French	so-so, indifferently
comme il faut	French	as it should be
contra	Latin	against
corps de ballet	French	dancers in a ballet
corps diplomatique	French	diplomatic circle
coup d'état	French	violent change of government
coup de grâce	French	finishing stroke
crème de la crème	French	the very best
cul-de-sac	French	blind alley

93

Term	Language	English meaning
de facto	Latin	in fact, really
de jure	Latin	by law
de luxe	French	of special quality
démodé	French	out of fashion
de novo	French	afresh, anew
dérangé	French	out of order
de rigueur	French	required by etiquette
de trop	French	not wanted, in the way
deus ex machina	Latin	last-minute solution, providential event that comes in the nick of time
Dieu et mon droit	French	God and my right (the motto of the British Sovereign)
double entendre	French	double meaning
embarras de richesse	French	more wealth than one knows what to do with
en bloc	French	in the mass
en famille	French	living informally with a family
en masse	French	in a body
en passant	French	by the way, in passing
en route	French	on the way
enfant terrible	French	little terror
entre nous	French	confidentially, between ourselves
ergo	Latin	therefore
esprit de corps	French	team spirit
et cetera	Latin	and so on
ex gratia	Latin	an act of grace
ex officio	Latin	by reason of office
fait accompli	French	an accomplished fact
faux pas	French	a blunder
floreat	Latin	let it flourish!
force majeure	French	irresistible compulsion
gourmet	French	one who likes good food
hic jacet	Latin	here lies
hoi polloi	Greek	the majority, the rabble
honi soi qui mal y pense	French	evil to him who evil thinks
honoris causa	Latin	for the sake of honour
hors de combat	French	out of a fight, disabled
hors d'oeuvre	French	dish served at beginning of meal

Term	Language	English meaning
ibidem (ibid.)	Latin	in the same book, chapter
ich dien	German	I serve (motto of the Prince of Wales)
id est (i.e.)	Latin	that is
idée fixé	French	fixed idea, obsession
idem .	Latin	the same
in camera	Latin	secretly, not in open court
in excelsis	Latin	in the highest
in extremis	Latin	in extreme difficulties, at the point of death
in loco parentis	Latin	in place of a parent
in memoriam	Latin	in memory
in perpetuum	Latin	for ever
in situ	Latin	in its place
in toto	Latin	as a whole, in entirety
inter alia	Latin	among others
ipso facto	Latin	by the fact itself
je ne sais quoi	French	I don't know what, indescribable
laisser-faire	French	to leave well alone
lèse-majesté	French	high treason
locum tenens	Latin	substitute, deputy
magnum opus	Latin	great work, an author's main work
maître d'hôtel	French	hotel manager, major-domo
maestro	Italian	great musical composer, teacher or conductor
mañana	Spanish	tomorrow
mariage de convenance	French	marriage of convenience
mise en scène	French	stage set
modus operandi	Latin	method of operation
modus vivendi	Latin	way of living
mot juste	French	exactly the right word
nil desperandum	Latin	don't despair
noblesse oblige	French	obligations of noble birth
nom de plume	French	pen-name
non compos mentis	Latin	of unsound mind
non sequitur	Latin	it does not follow
nota bene (NB)	Latin	note well
nouveau riche	French	someone with newly-acquired wealth

Term	Language	English meaning
opere citato	Latin	in the work named
outré	French	far out, eccentric, beyond the bounds of propriety
pace	Latin	by leave of
par excellence	French	of great excellence, eminently
par exemple	French	for example
pari passu	Latin	with equal pace, together
pax vobiscum	Latin	peace be with you!
per ardua ad astra	Latin	through hardship to the stars (R.A.F. motto)
per capita	Latin	per head
per centum	Latin	per hundred (usually shortened to per cent)
per diem	Latin	per day
persona grata	Latin	an acceptable person
persona non grata	Latin	person who is unacceptable
pièce de résistance	French	the best item
pied à terre	French	temporary place to stay at
poste restante	French	place (usually a post office) where letters can stay until called for
post meridiem	Latin	afternoon
post mortem	Latin	after death
prima ballerina	Italian	principal dancer in a ballet
prima donna	Italian	principal singer in an opera
prima facie	Latin	at first sight
pro rata	Latin	in proportion
pro tempore	Latin	for the time being
quid pro quo	Latin	tit for tat
quod erat demonstrandum	Latin	which was to be demonstrated (usually written Q.E.D.)
quod vide	Latin	which see (shortened to q.v.)
raison d'état	French	for reasons of State
raison d'être	French	reason for existence
regina	Latin	queen
requiescat in pace	Latin	rest in peace (R.I.P.)
répondez, s'il vous plaît	French	please reply (R.S.V.P.)

Term	Language	English meaning
résumé	French	shortened version, summary
risqué	French	risky, indelicate
sang-froid	French	self-possession
sans doute	French	without doubt
savoir faire	French	skill, tact
sic	Latin	thus, so
sine die	Latin	without a day being fixed, indefinitely
sine qua non	Latin	an indispensable condition
sobriquet	French	nickname
soi-disant	French	self-styled
soirée	French	evening party
sotto voce	Latin	in an undertone
status quo	Latin	as things stand, the same state
stet	Latin	let it stand, ignore correction
sub judice	Latin	under consideration (lawsuits etc.)
sub poena	Latin	under penalty
sub rosa	Latin	privately
table d'hôte	French	set meal
tempus fugit	Latin	time flies
terra firma	Latin	solid ground
tête-à-tête	French	conversation between two people
tour-de-force	French	feat of strength or skill
tout ensemble	French	thing viewed as a whole, altogether
trattoria	Italian	Italian eating-house
ubique	Latin	everywhere (motto of the Royal Artillery)
ultimo	Latin	last month
ultra vires	Latin	exceeding legal powers
verbatim	Latin	word for word
versus	Latin	against
vice versa	Latin	the other way round
vide	Latin	see
vis-à-vis	French	face to face
viva voce	Latin	orally
vol-au-vent	French	kind of puff-pastry pie
vox populi	Latin	public opinion
wagon-lit	French	sleeping-car on a railway

Abbreviations

A.A.	anti-aircraft; Automobile Association
A.A.A.	Amateur Athletic Association
A.B.	able-bodied seaman
a/c	account
A.D.	*anno Domini* (in the year of our Lord)
A.D.C.	aide-de-camp
ad fin.	*ad finem* (towards the end)
ad init.	*ad initium* (towards the beginning)
Adm.	Admiral
advt.	advertisement
A.F.A.	Amateur Football Association
A.M.	Air Ministry
a.m.	*ante meridiem* (before noon)
A. of F.	Admiral of the Fleet
arr.	arrival
Asst.	Assistant
A.T.C.	Air Training Corps
A.V.	Authorised Version (of the Bible)
avdp	avoirdupois
A.V.M.	Air Vice Marshal
A.W.O.L.	absent without leave
b.	born; bowled; bye
B.A.	Bachelor of Arts
B.A.O.R.	British Army of the Rhine
Bart.	Baronet
Bart's	St. Bartholomew's Hospital
B.C.	before Christ; British Columbia
B.Mus.	Bachelor of Music
B.R.	British Railways
B.Sc.	Bachelor of Science
C.	Centigrade
c.	caught; century; *circa*; colt
c.c.	cubic centimetre
C.E.	Church of England
ch., chap.	chapter
C.I.	Channel Islands
C.I.D.	Criminal Investigation Department
C.-in-C.	Commander-in-Chief
cm.	centimetre
C.O.D.	cash on delivery
Cons.	Conservative; consul
C.R.O.	Commonwealth Relations Office; Criminal Records Office
cu.	cubic
cwt.	hundredweight
d.	*denarius* (penny); date; daughter; died
D.A.	District Attorney

deg.	degree
dept.	department
dm.	decimetre
do.	ditto
doz.	dozen
Dr.	Doctor
dwt.	pennyweight
E.	east
Ed.	Edward; editor
EFTA	European Free Trade Association
e.g.	*exempli gratia* (for example)
E.R.	Elizabeth Regina (The Queen)
Esq.	Esquire
E.T.A.	estimated time of arrival
et seq.	*et sequentia* (and what follows)
F.	French, Fahrenheit
f.	feet; feminine; filly; foot; franc; free; from
F.A.	Football Association
F.B.I.	Federal Bureau of Investigation (US);
F.D.	*Fidei Defensor* (Defender of the Faith)
fl.	florin
Fr.	Father; French
fr.	franc
ft.	feet; foot
G.B.	Great Britain
G.B.S.	George Bernard Shaw
G.C.F.	greatest common factor
Gib.	Gibraltar
G.L.C.	Greater London Council
Glos.	Gloucestershire
gm.	gramme
G.M.T.	Greenwich Mean Time
G.P.	general practitioner (doctor)
G.P.O.	General Post Office
h. & c.	hot and cold water
H.C.F.	highest common factor
H.E.	His Excellency; high explosive
H.H.	His (or Her) Highness; His Holiness (the Pope)
Hi-Fi	high frequency
H.M.	His (or Her) Majesty
h.p.	horse power; hire purchase; half-pay; high pressure
H.Q.	headquarters
hr.	hour
H.R.H.	His (or Her) Royal Highness
I.C.B.M.	inter-continental ballistic missile
i.e.	*id est* (that is)

in.	inch
Inc.	Incorporated
inst.	instant (this month)
IOU	I owe you
I.Q.	intelligence quotient
I.R.A.	Irish Republican Army
I.T.A.	Independent Television Authority
J.A.	Judge Advocate
J.C.	Jesus Christ; Justice Clerk
J.P.	Justice of the Peace
kc.	kilocycle
kg.	kilogram
K.K.K.	Ku Klux Klan
km.	kilometre
K.O.	knock-out
K.R.	King's Regulations
Kt.	Knight
kw.	kilowatt
L	Latin; learner
l.	left; line; litre
Lab.	Labour
L.A.C.	leading aircraftman
Lat.	Latin
lat.	latitude
lb.	pound or pounds (weight)
l.c.	lower case
L.C.J.	Lord Chief Justice
L.C.M.	lowest common multiple
Lieut.	Lieutenant
log.	logarithm; logic
long.	longitude
l.p.	low pressure
L.S.D.	£.s.d. (pounds, shillings and pence)
L.S.O.	London Symphony Orchestra
Lt.	Lieutenant
l.t.	low tension
L.T.A.	Lawn Tennis Association
Ltd.	Limited
M.	Monsieur
m.	maiden (over); male; married; masculine; metre; mile; minute; million
matric.	matriculation
M.B.	Bachelor of Medicine
M.C.	Master of Ceremonies
M.C.C.	Marylebone Cricket Club
M.D.	Doctor of Medicine; mentally deficient
Messrs.	plural of Mr.
met.	meteorology
Metro.	Paris Underground Railway

M.F.H.	Master of Foxhounds
mg.	milligram
Mgr.	Monseigneur
M.I.	Military Intelligence (as in M.I.5)
misc.	miscellaneous; miscellany
Mlle.	Mademoiselle
MM.	Messieurs
Mme.	Madame
M.N.	Merchant Navy
M.N.I.	Ministry of National Insurance
M.O.	mass observation; Medical Officer; money order
M.O.H.	Medical Officer of Health
M.P.	Member of Parliament; military police
m.p.g., m.p.h.	miles per gallon; miles per hour
Mr.	Mister
Mrs.	originally Mistress, now title of married woman
Ms.	Mrs. or Miss
MSS.	manuscripts
N.	navigator; new; north
n.	nominative; neuter; noon; noun
N.A.A.F.I.	Navy, Army and Air Force Institutes
N.A.T.O.	North Atlantic Treaty Organisation
N.B.	*nota bene* (note well)
N.F.U.	National Farmers' Union
No.	number
nom.	nominal; nominative
N.O.P.	National Opinion Poll
n.p.	new paragraph
N.T.	New Testament
N.Y.C.	New York City
N.Z.	New Zealand
O.H.M.S.	On Her (or His) Majesty's Service
O.K.	all correct
O.T.	Old Testament
oz.	ounce
p.	page; particle; past; pence; perch
p.a.	*per annum* (per year)
par.	paragraph
P.A.Y.E.	Pay As You Earn
Paym (-Gen)	Paymaster (-General)
P.C.	Police Constable; postcard; Privy Councillor
p.c.	per cent; postcard
per pro.	*per procurationem* (by proxy, on behalf of)
P.G.	paying guest
pl.	place; plate; plural
P.L.A.	Port of London Authority

P.M.	Prime Minister; Provost Marshal
p.m.	*post meridiem* (afternoon),
	post mortem (after death)
P.M.G.	Postmaster-General; Paymaster-General
p.m.h.	production per man-hour
P.O.S.B.	Post Office Savings Bank
P.O.W.	prisoner-of-war
pp.	pages
P.P.S.	*post postscriptum* (further postscript)
Pref.	Preface
Pres.	President
P.R.O.	Public Relations Officer
Prof.	Professor
pro tem.	*pro tempore* (for the time being)
P.S.	Police Sergeant; postscript
Ps.	Psalm
P.T.O.	please turn over
Q.	Queen
Q.B.	Queen's Bench
Q.C.	Queen's Counsel
Q.E.D.	*quod erat demonstrandum* (which was to be demonstrated)
Q.S.	Quarter Sessions
R.	*Regina* (Queen); *Rex* (King); river; railway; right; run; rupee
R.A.	Royal Academy; Royal Academician; Royal Artillery
R.A.C.	Royal Automobile Club
R.A.D.A.	Royal Academy of Dramatic Art
R.A.M.	Royal Academy of Music
R.C.	Roman Catholic
R.C.A.F.	Royal Canadian Air Force
R.C.M.P.	Royal Canadian Mounted Police
R.D.	refer to drawer
R.D.C.	Rural District Council
recd.	received
repr.	represented; reprinted
Revd.	Reverend
R.I.B.A.	Royal Institute of British Architects
R.I.P.	*requiescat in pace* (rest in peace)
R.N.L.I.	Royal National Lifeboat Institution
R.S.A.	Royal Society of Arts
R.S.P.C.A.	Royal Society for the Prevention of Cruelty to Animals
R.S.V.P.	*répondez s'il vous plaît* (please reply)
Rt. Hon.	Right Honourable
Rt. Rev.	Right Reverend
R.V.	Revised Version (of Bible)
S.	Saint; soprano; south; submarines

s.	second; shilling; singular; son
Salop	Shropshire
S.E.A.T.O.	South-east Asia Treaty Organisation
Sgt.	Sergeant
s.h.p.	shaft horse-power
S.O.S.	distress signal; possibly abbreviation of Save Oh Save! or Save Our Souls!
sov.	sovereign
S.P.C.K.	Society for Promoting Christian Knowledge
S.P.G.	Society for the Propagation of the Gospel
sp. gr.	specific gravity
sq.	square
S.R.N.	State Registered Nurse
SS.	Saints
St.	Saint; strait; street
sup.	superlative; *supra* (above)
t.	ton
T.B.	torpedo-boat; tubercle bacillus; tuberculosis
T.N.T.	trinitrotoluene (explosive)
T.T.	teetotaller; Tourist Trophy; tuberculin tested
T.U.C.	Trades Union Congress
U.	universal
U.K.	United Kingdom
ult.	*ultimo* (last month)
U.N.	United Nations
U.N.E.S.C.O.	United Nations Educational, Scientific & Cultural Organisation
U.N.O.	United Nations Organisation
U.S.A.	United States of America
U.S.S.R.	Union of Soviet Socialist Republics
v.	verse; versus; volt
V.C.	Vice-Chancellor, Victoria Cross
VE	Victory in Europe (VE day, May 8, 1945)
V.H.F.	very high frequency
V.I.P.	very important person
W.	Welsh; west
w.	watt; wicket; wide; wife; with
W.C.	water closet
W.I.	West Indies; Women's Institute
W.P.	weather permitting
W.R.V.S.	Women's Royal Voluntary Service
wt.	weight
Xmas	Christmas
Y.H.A.	Youth Hostels Association
Y.M.C.A.	Young Men's Christian Association
yr.	year; your
Y.W.C.A.	Young Women's Christian Association

Meanings and origins of some familiar words and phrases
There are many words and phrases commonly used today which go back hundreds of years. Here are some of the more familiar ones, with their meanings and probable origins:

A.1
Meaning: Excellent, first-rate
Origin: British ships are built to Lloyds Register of Shipping Regulations. One built to conform to the strictest regulations is classed A. 1. Hence, of the highest quality.

Baker's dozen
Meaning: 13 instead of 12.
Origin: From the habit of bakers at one time of giving 13 rolls to the dozen to avoid being fined for selling underweight.

Bury the hatchet
Meaning: To make up a quarrel.
Origin: Red Indians, when they made peace with their enemies, would bury their weapons to show their good faith and to ensure that the war would not break out again.

Cock and bull story
Meaning: Story which cannot be believed.
Origin: A Papal Bull is an edict made by the Pope and sealed with the Pope's seal, which bears a figure of St. Peter and a cock. After the Reformation, Papal Bulls went unheeded, and consequently any incredible tale is a "cock and bull story".

Cold shoulder
Meaning: To ignore someone.
Origin: To discourage unwelcome visitors, a hostess merely served them with the remains of the joint, a fairly plain hint that they were not to call again.

Feather in one's cap
Meaning: Something one may be proud of.
Origin: From the habit of Red Indians of sticking a feather in their head-dresses for every enemy they had slain.

Hobson's choice
Meaning: A choice that is really no choice at all, since the alternative would be nothing.
Origin: In the 17th century, Tobias Hobson kept a stable at Cambridge, from which he hired out horses. Although all his horses were ostensibly for hire, he would allow only the one nearest the door to be chosen, so that his horses were ridden in strict rotation. Any objection was met with the firm comment, "It's that or none."

Knuckle under, to
Meaning: To submit or to yield.
Origin: In Anglo-Saxon and Mediaeval English, the knuckle refers to the knee-joint as well as the finger-joints. To knuckle under, therefore, meant to bow the knee.

Mad as a hatter

Meaning: Crazy.

Origin: The phrase has nothing to do with hatters nor with madness. It was originally "mad as an atter." Atter was the Anglo-Saxon word for a viper or adder, and mad meant venomous. The expression thus meant as venomous as a viper.

On tenterhooks

Meaning: To be taut with anxiety.

Origin: After weaving, cloth is fixed by hooks to a frame and stretched so that it will dry evenly, without shrinking. The hooks are known as tenterhooks.

Post haste

Meaning: In a hurry.

Origin: In coaching days, a person wishing to get somewhere quickly would arrange for a relay of horses at the posting stations along his route.

Raining cats and dogs

Meaning: Pouring with rain.

Origin: Probably a corruption of an obsolete French word, *catadoupe*, which means a heavy fall of water.

Rule of thumb

Meaning: Rule based on experience or practice.

Origin: It is said to have arisen from the habit of brewers in Yorkshire of dipping their thumbs into the vat to determine the heat of the liquor.

That's the ticket

Meaning: That's just right.

Origin: A corruption of the French *étiquette* meaning that is what you should do.

Uncle Sam

Meaning: The United States of America.

Origin: The story goes that a man named Elbert Anderson of New York had a store yard on the Hudson River. A Government inspector named Samuel Wilson, who was always known as Uncle Sam, used to examine the stores, marking the packages he had passed EA-US, the initials of Elbert Anderson and the United States. One of the employees was asked what the initials stood for and replied facetiously that the US stood for Uncle Sam. The story spread and soon Uncle Sam became the nickname for America, just as John Bull is for England.

White elephant

Meaning: Something that is quite useless and often expensive to maintain.

Origin: In Siam, a white elephant was regarded as sacred. When the King of Siam wanted to be rid of the services of one of his courtiers, he would make him a present of a white elephant. The cost of keeping the animal usually ruined the poor man.

White feather, to show the
Meaning: To be a coward.
Origin: From cock-fighting days, when no true-bred gaming cocks ever had a white feather. If a cock had one, he was a crossbred and probably no great fighter.

Yankee
Meaning: An American.
Origin: From the first attempts by the North-American Indians to pronounce the word, English.

Famous Women

Anderson, Anna. Woman, now living in the Black Forest, who, for more than 30 years, has claimed to be the Grand Duchess Anastasia Nikolaievna Romanov (1901-? 1918), daughter of Tsar Nicholas II of Russia. Anastasia is believed to have died with the rest of the Romanovs when the Russian Royal Family was executed by the Bolsheviks in 1918. Anna Anderson claims a miraculous escape, but she has so far failed to establish the truth of her assertion. A Hamburg court finally rejected her claim in 1961.

Astor, Nancy Witcher Langhorne, Viscountess (1879-1964), wife of English politician, Viscount Astor, born in Virginia, U.S.A. First woman Member of Parliament in Britain when she took her seat in the House of Commons in 1919.

Auriol, Jacqueline (1918-), French woman pilot, who broke the women's jet speed record in 1955 by flying at 1151 km. an hour in a French Mystère.

Austen, Jane (1775-1817), English novelist, born in Steventon, Hants, the daughter of a rector. She wrote six great novels, SENSE AND SENSIBILITY (published 1811), PRIDE AND PREJUDICE (1813), MANSFIELD PARK (1814), EMMA (1815), PERSUASION (1818) and NORTHANGER ABBEY (1818).

Beale, Dorothea (1831-1906), pioneer of education for women; born in London; Principal of Cheltenham Ladies' College from 1858.

Beeton, Mrs (Isabella Mary Mayson (1836-1865), famous for her writing on cookery. Her book HOUSEHOLD MANAGEMENT, published in

1859 to 1860, made her name a household word.

Bernhardt, Sarah (born Henriette Rosine Bernhard 1844-1923), greatest tragic actress of her day; born in Paris.

Bloomer, Amelia (1818-1894), née Jenks, born at Homer, New York; championed women's right to wear trousers. The full trousers she wore came to be called bloomers.

Boadicea (1st century, A.D.), British warrior-queen, wife of Prasutagus, king of the Iceni, a tribe inhabiting the part of England now known as Norfolk and Suffolk. Led a large army against the Roman occupiers of Britain with great success until she was finally defeated by Suetonius Paulinus, the Roman governor of Britain, and took poison.

Buss, Frances Mary (1827-1894), with Dorothea Beale a pioneer of education for women. Founded the North London Collegiate School for Ladies.

Browning, Elizabeth Barrett (1806-1861), English poet, born at Coxhoe Hall, Durham. Married the English poet, Robert Browning, in 1846. She was an invalid for many years following a spinal injury when she was 15. Suffered from an over-possessive father.

Brontë, the name of three sisters, all novelists: *Anne (1820-1849)* wrote under the pseudonym Acton Bell, best-known novel is AGNES GREY (published 1845); *Charlotte (1816-1855)*, pseudonym Currer Bell, best-known work JANE EYRE (1847), married her father's curate, Mr. Nicholls, in 1854; *Emily Jane (1818-1848),* pseudonym Ellis Bell, best-known work WUTHERING HEIGHTS (1847).

Calamity Jane, nickname of Martha Jane Burke (c. 1852-1903), American frontierswoman known for her eccentric ways. She usually wore men's clothes and was a skilful rider and shot.

Campbell, Mrs Patrick (née Beatrice Stella Tanner 1865-1940), famous actress; creator of Eliza Doolittle in Shaw's PYGMALION in 1914.

Cavell, Edith (1866-1915), nurse who tended the wounded in Brussels in 1914 to 1915. Executed by the Germans on October 12, 1915, for helping Belgian and Allied fugitives.

Colette, Sidonie Gabrielle (1873-1954), French novelist who wrote, among other things, GIGI.

Darling, Grace (1815-1842), lighthouse-keeper's daughter; famous for her rescue of the survivors of the FORFARSHIRE, wrecked off the Farne Islands, the Northumbrian coast, in 1838.

Du Barry, Marie Jeanne Gomard de Vaubernier, Comtesse (1741-1793), daughter of a dressmaker, became the favourite of the French King Louis XV. Tried before the Revolutionary Tribunal for having wasted the treasures of the state and worn mourning for the late king, was found guilty and sent to the guillotine.

Eliot, George (pen-name of Mary Ann Evans 1819-1880), English novelist; works include ADAM BEDE (1859) and THE MILL ON THE FLOSS (1860).

Elizabeth, Queen of Bohemia (1596-1662), "The Winter Queen", eldest daughter of King James I of England and VI of Scotland, grandmother of King George I of England.

Ferrier, Kathleen (1912-1953), famous English contralto singer, born in Higher Walton, Lancs. Sang throughout Europe and America.

Fitzherbert, Mrs (née Maria Anne Smythe 1756-1837), secretly married to King George IV while he was Prince of Wales. The marriage was declared invalid under the Royal Marriage Act of 1772 because it had taken place without King George III's consent.

Fonteyn, Dame Margot (née Margaret Hookham 1919-), famous English ballerina, born in Reigate, Surrey. Married Emilio Arias, Panamanian Ambassador to Britain in 1955 and was created a D.B.E. in 1956.

Fry, Elizabeth (1780-1845), prison reformer. By birth and marriage (she was the daughter of a rich Quaker banker, John Gurney), she was a member of two leading Quaker families. In 1813, she visited Newgate Prison and found 300 women, tried and untried, with their children, herded together in squalid conditions. Thenceforth, she devoted her life to prison reform both in this country and abroad.

Gaskell, Mrs Elizabeth Gleghorn (1810-1865), English novelist, born in Chelsea, London. Her most famous novel is CRANFORD (published 1853).

Godiva, wife of Leofric, Earl of Chester (11th century). According to the legend, she forced her husband to rescind the heavy tax he had imposed on the citizens of Coventry by riding naked through the market-place.

Greenaway, Kate (1846-1901), English artist who became well-known for her charming illustrations of children.

Joan of Arc, St. (c. 1412-1431), French patriot and martyr, who led French resistance against the English. She was put on trial for heresy and sorcery by a court of the Inquisition, found guilty and burnt at the stake on May 30, 1431.

Johnson, Amy (1903-1941), English aviator, born at Kingston-upon-Hull. She was the first woman to be granted an Air Ministry's ground engineer's licence. In 1930, she flew solo from England to Australia, breaking the record as far as Karachi. She married another famous flyer, James Mollison, whom she divorced in 1938.

Keller, Helen Adams (1880-1968), born in Alabama, U.S.A.; became deaf and blind at 19 months, but, taught by Miss Anne Sullivan, she learned to speak, graduated B.A. in 1904 and became well-known as a lecturer and writer.

Kemble, Fanny (1809-1893), Shakespearean actress and member of a famous theatrical family. Married an American, Pierce Butler, in 1834 and was divorced in 1848.

Langtry, Emily Charlotte (1852-1929), famous actress and theatre-manager; acted under the stage-name Lillie Langtry, nicknamed the Jersey Lily. She was born in Jersey and was one of the most famous beauties of her time.

Macdonald, Flora (1722-1790), Scottish heroine, born in South Uist.

After the 1745 Jacobite Rebellion, she assisted Bonnie Prince Charlie, the Young Pretender, to escape from the English. She married the son of Macdonald of Kingsburgh in 1750.

Marie Antoinette Josephe Jeanne (1755-1793), Queen of France, wife of King Louis XVI, whom she married when he was Dauphin in 1770. Following the French Revolution, she was imprisoned in the Conciergerie, brought to trial before the Revolutionary Tribunal and guillotined on October 16, 1793.

Markova, Alicia (née Lilian Alicia Marks (1910-). English prima ballerina; born in London, became a member of the Diaghilev company in 1924. Her most famous partnership was with Anton Dolin. She was prima ballerina with the Festival Ballet company from 1950 to 1952.

Mata Hari, stage-name of Margarete Gertrude Zelle (1876-1917), Dutch spy who became a dancer in France; was found guilty of spying for the Germans and shot in Paris.

Melba, Dame Nellie (1859-1931), Australian prima donna; born at Melbourne, appeared at Covent Garden in 1888. Her soprano voice won her universal fame. She was created a D.B.E. in 1927.

Mistinguett, stage-name of Jeanne Marie Bourgeois (1874-1956), French dancer and actress who was one of the most popular music-hall stars between 1900 and 1930.

Mitford, Nancy (1904-), English writer; author of, among other books, PURSUIT OF LOVE (1945), and LOVE IN A COLD CLIMATE (1949). In NOBLESSE OBLIGE (1956), she originated "U" and "non-U" as a means of classifying what is and is not English upper-class behaviour and speech.

Montespan, Françoise Athénias, Marquise de (1641-1707), French favourite of King Louis XIV. Daughter of the Duc de Mortemart, married the Marquis de Montespan in 1663. She left the French court and retired to a convent in 1687.

Moses, Anna Mary, known as Grandma Moses (1860-1961), American primitive artist, born in Washington County, New York. Started painting at the age of 75 and achieved great success.

Nightingale, Florence (1820-1910), hospital reformer, born at Florence. During the Crimean War, she organised a nursing department at Scutari, tending 10,000 wounded and sick men, many of whom died because of the appalling sanitary conditions. Florence Nightingale was determined to change this and she spent many years on Army sanitary reform, the improvement of nursing and public health in India. She founded an institution for the training of nurses at St. Thomas's Hospital and King's College Hospital.

Orczy, Baroness Emmumska (1865-1947) British novelist born in Hungary. Created one of the most romantic heroes in fiction, Sir Percy Blakeney, in THE SCARLET PIMPERNEL, her first book, published in 1905.

Parker, Dorothy (1903-), American satirical writer, famed for her pertinent sayings and verse.

Pavlova, Anna (1885-1931), Russian ballerina, born at St. Peters-

Florence Nightingale

burg. Formed her own ballet company in 1909.

Pocohontas (1595-1617), Red Indian princess, daughter of Powhattan, an Indian chief; twice saved the life of Captain John Smith, who was on an expedition to colonise Virginia, U.S.A. She became a Christian, married an Englishman, John Rolfe, in 1613 and came to England in 1616.

Pompadour, Jeanne Antoinette Poisson, Marquise de (1721-1764), born in Paris, a woman famed for her grace, wit and beauty. She became a favourite of King Louis XV and for 20 years exerted great influence on affairs of state. She founded the Ecole Militaire and the royal china factory at Sèvres.

Potter, Beatrix (1866-1943), creator of the PETER RABBIT books for children, which she illustrated herself.

Rossetti, Christina (1830-1894), English poetess, born in London. A devout Christian, she wrote mainly religious poetry.

Sand, George (pen-name of Amandine Aurore Lucie Dupin, Baronne Dudevant 1804-1876), French novelist, born in Paris. A friend of the composer Chopin, she wrote more than 100 books.

Sewell, Anna (1820-1878), British novelist, born in Yarmouth, who is remembered for the most famous fictional story about horses ever written, BLACK BEAUTY (1877).

Siddons, Sarah (1755-1831), English actress, born at Brecon, the daughter of Roger Kemble. Her stage career began in early childhood with her father's travelling theatrical company and she developed into the greatest tragedienne the English stage has ever known.

Stopes, Marie Carmichael (1880-1958), born near Dorking, Surrey; pioneer of family planning. Her book on the subject, MARRIED LOVE, provoked enormous controversy when it was published in 1918.

Stowe, Harriet Elizabeth Beecher (1811-1896), American novelist, born at Litchfield, Connecticut. She earned fame through her book, UNCLE TOM'S CABIN (1825), which aroused tremendous anti-slavery feeling in the Northern States.

Terry, Dame Ellen Alice (1848-1928), English actress, born at Coventry. As the leading Shakespearean actress of her day, she dominated the London stage from 1878 to 1902 in partnership with Henry Irving.

Tussaud, Marie (née Grosholtz 1760-1850), modeller in wax; born in Berne, Switzerland. She came to England in 1800 and toured this country with her waxwork models. In 1835, she set up a permanent waxwork exhibition in Baker Street. It burned down in 1925 and in 1928 was re-opened on its present site. Some of her own models can still be seen at Madame Tussaud's.

Useful Tables

British Weights and Measures

Length

12 inches	= 1 foot
3 feet	= 1 yard
5½ yards	= 1 rod, pole or perch
22 yards	= 1 chain=100 links
10 chains	= 1 furlong
220 yards	= 1 furlong
8 furlongs	= 1 mile=1760 yards

Additional measures of length

4 inches	= 1 hand (used in measuring the height of animals, especially horses)
6 feet	= 1 fathom
120 fathoms	= 1 cable=240 yards
6,080 feet	= 1 U.K. nautical mile
6,076 feet	= 1 International nautical mile
(Note: 1 knot	= 1 nautical mile per hour)

Area

144 square inches	= 1 square foot
9 square feet	= 1 square yard
1,210 square yards	= 1 rood
4 roods	= 1 acre=4,840 square yards
640 acres	= 1 square mile

Volume

1,728 cubic inches	= 1 cubic foot
27 cubic feet	= 1 cubic yard

Weight (Avoirdupois)

27·344 grains	= 1 dram
16 drams	= 1 ounce
16 ounces	= 1 pound=7,000 grains
14 pounds	= 1 stone
28 pounds (2 stones)	= 1 quarter
4 quarters (112 pounds)	= 1 hundredweight
20 hundredweight	= 1 ton

Weight (Troy—used for measuring gold and silver)

24 grains	= 1 pennyweight
20 pennyweights	= 1 ounce Troy

Weight (Apothecaries'—used for measuring drugs)
20 grains	= 1 scruple
3 scruples	= 1 drachm
8 drachms	= 1 ounce

(Note: 1 ounce Troy is the same as 1 ounce Apothecaries'.)

Capacity
4 gills	= 1 pint
20 fluid ounces	= 1 pint
2 pints	= 1 quart
4 quarts	= 1 gallon=8 pints
2 gallons	= 1 peck
4 pecks	= 1 bushel } Used for measuring
8 bushels	= 1 quarter } solids

Capacity (Apothecaries')
60 minims	= 1 fluid drachm
8 fluid drachms	= 1 fluid ounce
5 fluid ounces	= 1 gill
4 gills	= 1 pint
8 pints	= 1 gallon

Angles
60 seconds (")	= 1 minute (')
60 minutes	= 1 degree (°)
90 degrees	= right angle or quadrant
4 right angles	= 1 circle (360°)

Time
60 seconds	= 1 minute
60 minutes	= 1 hour
24 hours	= 1 day
7 days	= 1 week
52 weeks and 1 day	= 1 year
365 days	= 1 year

Metric Weights and Measures

Length
10 millimetres	= 1 centimetre
10 centimetres	= 1 decimetre
10 decimetres	= 1 metre=100 centimetres
10 metres	= 1 dekametre
10 dekametres	= 1 hectometre
10 hectometres	= 1 kilometre=1,000 metres

Area

100 square metres	= 1 are
10 ares	= 1 dekare
10 dekares	= 1 hectare
100 hectares	= 1 square kilometre

Weight

10 milligrams	= 1 centigram
10 centigrams	= 1 decigram
10 decigrams	= 1 gramme
10 grammes	= 1 dekagram
10 dekagrams	= 1 hectogram
10 hectograms	= 1 kilogram = 1,000 grammes
10 kilograms	= 1 myriagram
10 myriagrams	= 1 quintal
10 quintals	= 1 tonne = 1,000 kilograms

Capacity

10 millilitres	= 1 centilitre
10 centilitres	= 1 decilitre
10 decilitres	= 1 litre
10 litres	= 1 dekalitre
10 dekalitres	= 1 hectolitre

Conversion Tables (English to Metric)

Length

1 inch	= 2.540 centimetres
1 foot	= 30.480 centimetres
1 yard	= 0.914 metres
1 mile	= 1.609 kilometres

Area

1 square inch	= 6.452 square centimetres
1 square foot	= 9.290 square decimetres
1 square yard	= 0.836 square metres
1 acre	= 0.405 hectares
1 square mile	= 2.590 square kilometres

Volume

1 cubic inch	= 16.387 cubic centimetres
1 cubic foot	= 0.028 cubic metres
1 cubic yard	= 0.765 cubic metres

Capacity

1 Imperial pint	= 0.568 litres

1 Imperial quart	= 1.136 litres
1 Imperial gallon	= 4.456 litres
1 bushel	= 3.367 decalitres

Weight

1 grain	= 0.065 grammes
1 ounce (avoirdupois)	= 28.350 grammes
1 ounce (Troy)	= 31.104 grammes
1 pound (avoirdupois)	= 0.454 kilograms
1 hundredweight	= 50.800 kilograms
1 ton	= 1.016 tonnes

Conversion Tables (Metric to English)

Length

1 millimetre	= 0.0394 inches
1 centimetre	= 0.394 inches
1 decimetre	= 3.937 inches
1 metre	= 39.370 inches or 3.281 feet or 1.094 yards
1 kilometre	= 0.621 miles

(Note: for quick conversion of kilometres to miles, multiply the number of kilometres by 5 and divide by 8.)

Area

1 square centimetre	= 0.155 square inches
1 square metre	= 10.764 square feet or 1.196 square yards
1 are	= 119.600 square yards
1 hectare	= 2.471 acres
1 square kilometre	= 0.386 square miles

Volume

1 cubic centimetre	= 0.061 cubic inches
1 cubic metre	= 35.317 cubic feet or 1.308 cubic yards

Capacity

1 decilitre	= 0.176 pints
1 litre	= 1.760 pints
1 decalitre	= 2.200 gallons
1 hectolitre	= 2.750 bushels

Weight

1 gramme	= 15.432 grains
1 hectogram	= 3.527 ounces
1 kilogram	= 2.205 pounds
1 tonne	= 0.984 tons

Mach Numbers

If you have heard or read any reports on supersonic aircraft, you may have noticed the term Mach (pronounced Mark) when reference is made to the aircraft's speed. A Mach Number is the ratio of an object's speed to the local speed of sound in similar surrounding conditions. Mach 1.0 at sea-level at standard pressure and temperature is the equivalent of 1,225 km. per hour. In the stratosphere, however, the equivalent to Mach 1.0 is some 163 km/h slower at 1,062 km/h. The term Mach is named after Ernst Mach, a professor of physics at Prague, Czechoslovakia, who died in 1916. Stratospheric Mach Numbers in terms of km/h are shown in the table below:

Mach 1.0	1,061.78 km/h	Mach 5.0	5,308.92 km/h
Mach 2.0	2,123.57 km/h	Mach 6.0	6,370.70 km/h
Mach 3.0	3,185.35 km/h	Mach 7.0	7,432.49 km/h
Mach 4.0	4,247.13 km/h		

Temperatures

The two principal temperature scales are Centigrade and Fahrenheit. The Centigrade scale is in use on the Continent and is gradually being introduced in Great Britain in preference to the Fahrenheit scale. The Meteorological Office, for example, now use Centigrade temperatures in all their weather forecasts. Fahrenheit markings, however, are the most familiar to us and are found on most domestic thermometers. The Fahrenheit scale, which was named after Gilbert Daniel Fahrenheit, a German physicist who died in 1736, defines freezing point as 32° and boiling point as 212°. The Centigrade scale is simpler, with 0° as freezing point and 100° for boiling point. To convert a Fahrenheit reading to Centigrade, subtract 32, multiply by 5 and divide by 9. Centigrade is converted to Fahrenheit by multiplying by 9, dividing by 5 and adding 32. The letters F. and C. following the temperature reading denote which scale is being used. Here are some useful comparisons:

Absolute Zero	—273.16°C.	—459.69°F.
Point of Equality	—40.0°C.	—40.0°F.
Zero Fahrenheit	—17.8°C.	
Zero Centigrade		32.0°F.
Freezing Point	0.0°C.	32.0°F.
Boiling Point	100.0°C.	212.0°F.
100° Centigrade		212.0°F.
100° Fahrenheit	37.8°C.	
Normal Temperature of Human Blood	36.9°C.	98.4°F.

Mathematics: Symbols

  . decimal point   < less than

=	equals	×	multiplied by
≠	does not equal	÷	divided by
≡	congruent to	%	per cent
+	plus	‰	per thousand
−	minus	≥	equal to or greater than
±	plus or minus	≤	equal to or less than
Δ	triangle	≏	approximately equal to
>	greater than	≮	not less than
∥	parallel to	√	square root
#	not parallel to	rⁿ	r to the power of n
≯	not greater than		

No.	Square	Cube	Square Root	Cube Root	Reciprocal
1	1	1	1.0	1.0	1.0
2	4	8	1.414	1.26	0.5
3	9	27	1.732	1.414	0.3333
4	16	64	2.0	1.587	0.25
5	25	125	2.236	1.71	0.2
6	36	216	2.449	1.817	0.1667
7	49	343	2.646	1.913	0.1429
8	64	512	2.828	2.0	0.125
9	81	729	3.0	2.08	0.1111
10	100	1,000	3.162	2.154	0.1
11	121	1,331	3.317	2.224	0.0909
12	144	1,728	3.464	2.289	0.0833
13	169	2,197	3.606	2.351	0.0769
14	196	2,744	3.742	2.41	0.0714
15	225	3,375	3.873	2.466	0.0667
16	256	4,096	4.0	2.52	0.0625
17	289	4,913	4.123	2.571	0.0588
18	324	5,832	4.243	2.621	0.0556
19	361	6,859	4.359	2.668	0.0526
20	400	8,000	4.472	2.714	0.05
25	625	15,625	5.0	2.924	0.04
30	900	27,000	5.477	3.107	0.0333
35	1,225	42,875	5.916	3.271	0.0286
40	1,600	64,000	6.325	3.42	0.025
45	2,025	91,125	6.708	3.557	0.0222
50	2,500	125,000	7.071	3.681	0.02

Mathematical Formulae

Triangle
Area = ½ base × height

Square
Area = side × side

Circle
($\pi = 3{\cdot}14159$)
Diameter (d) = 2 × radius (r) = 2r
Circumference = $2\pi r$ or πd

Area = πr^2 or $\dfrac{\pi d^2}{4}$

Quadrant = 90°. 4 quadrants = 360° = circle

Sphere

Volume = $\dfrac{4\pi r^3}{3}$ Surface area = $4\pi r^2$

Cone

Volume = $\dfrac{\pi r^2 h}{3}$

Curved surface area = πr × slant height (l) or $\pi r l$

Cylinder

Curved surface area = $2\pi rh$ Volume = $\pi r^2 h$
Total surface area = $2\pi rh + 2\pi r = 2\pi r(h + r)$

Ellipse
(major axis = 2a, minor axis = 2b)   Area = πab

Pyramid
(x = length of side, m = slant height)

Volume = $\dfrac{(\pi^2 h)}{3}$ Surface area = $x^2 + 2mx$

Trapezium
Area = $h \times \dfrac{\text{(parallel sides added together)}}{2}$

The Greek Alphabet
The word "alphabet" is derived from the first two letters of the Greek alphabet. It is included in the mathematical section because so many of its letters are used as mathematical symbols. Pi (π) is a good example.

Alpha	A	α	Nu	N	ν
Beta	B	β	Xi	Ξ	ξ
Gamma	Γ	γ	Omicron	O	o
Delta	Δ	δ	Pi	Π	π
Epsilon	E	ϵ	Rho	P	ρ

Zeta	Z	ζ	Sigma	Σ	σ, ς
Eta	H	η	Tau	T	τ
Theta	Θ	Θ	Upsilon	Y	υ
Iota	I	ι	Phi	Φ	ρ
Kappa	K	κ	Chi	X	χ
Lambda	Λ	λ	Psi	Ψ	ψ
Mu	M	μ	Omega	Ω	ω

Roman Numerals

Rules

When a letter is repeated, the value of the number is increased by the value of that letter. e.g., XX=20, CCC=300, MMM=3,000.

Letters are placed in order of value, the letter of smaller value increasing the amount of the whole number by the amount of the smaller. e.g., VII=7, LXII=62.

A letter placed before another letter of greater value decreases the number by the value of the smaller letter. e.g., IX=9, XL=40, CM=900, MCM=1,900.

A bar placed over a letter or group of letters multiplies the value by 1,000. e.g., $\overline{X}$=10,000, $\overline{XL}$=40,000.

I—	1	XX—	20	MCC—	1,200
II—	2	XXX—	30	MCCC—	1,300
III—	3	XL—	40	MCD—	1,400
IV or IIII—	4	L—	50	MD—	1,500
V—	5	LX—	60	MDC—	1,600
VI—	6	LXX—	70	MDCC—	1,700
VII—	7	LXXX—	80	MDCCC—	1,800
VIII—	8	XC—	90	MCM—	1,900
IX—	9	C—	100	MM—	2,000
X—	10	CC—	200	MMM—	3,000
XI—	11	CCC—	300	$\overline{IV}$—	4,000
XII—	12	CD or CCCC—	400	$\overline{V}$—	5,000
XIII—	13	D—	500	$\overline{X}$—	10,000
XIV—	14	DC—	600	$\overline{L}$—	50,000
XV—	15	DCC—	700	$\overline{C}$—	100,000
XVI—	16	DCCC—	800	$\overline{D}$—	500,000
XVII—	17	CM—	900	$\overline{M}$—	1,000,000
XVIII—	18	M—	1,000		
XIX—	19	MC—	1,100		

Quick guide to the value of Roman numerals:

I=1, V=5, X=10, L=50, C=100, D=500, M=1,000. Dates on old tombstones are often written in Roman numerals. To calculate the year, start from the left and work towards the right adding the values together as you go. For example, if the year is given as MDCCLXXXIV, this equals M+D+C+C+L+X+X+X+(V—I) which equals 1,000+500+100+100+50+10+10+10+(5−1), which works out as 1784.

1974 in Roman numerals=MCMLXXIV.
1975 in Roman numerals=MCMLXXV.
1976 in Roman numerals=MCMLXXVI.

Binary numbers
In any counting system, all numbers are represented by symbols or by a combination of symbols. Our normal method of counting is by the decimal system, which has ten symbols—0, 1, 2, 3, 4, 5, 6, 7, 8 and 9. Each of those symbols represents a number which is 1 more than the preceding one. We add 1 to 2 to get 3, 1 to 3 to get 4, and so on. But when we add 1 to 9, we find that there is no symbol for ten (as there is, for example, in Roman numerals, where the symbol is X). So we have to go back to the beginning again and, carrying 1 into the next column to indicate that 9 has been reached, we use a combination of symbols—i.e., 1 and 0, making 10.

The binary system has only two symbols, 0 and 1. The symbols 2 to 9 just do not exist. Whereas the limit in the decimal system is reached at 9, the limit in binary is reached at 1. But the difficulty is overcome in the same way—we put down 0 and carry 1 to the next column, to indicate that 1 has been reached.

The table below is a conversion scale from the ten-scale (decimal) to the two-scale (binary).

decimal	binary	decimal	binary
1	1	*16	10000
2	10	17	10001
3	11	18	10010
*4	100	19	10011
5	101	20	10100
6	110	21	10101
7	111	22	10110
*8	1000	23	10111
9	1001	24	11000
10	1010	*32	100000
11	1011	*64	1000000
12	1100	100	1100100
13	1101	*128	10000000
14	1110	*256	100000000
15	1111	*512	1000000000

In the table above, certain numbers in the decimal column have been starred. These numbers are powers of 2. Thus:

$2^1 = 2$ to the power of 1.
$2^2 = 2$ to the power of 2, or 2×2, which equals 4.
$2^3 = 2$ to the power of 3, or $2 \times 2 \times 2 = 8$.
Any number to the power of $0 = 1$. Thus: $2^0 = 1$.

The number of 0's after 1, in the binary system, indicates the power to which 2 is raised. Thus: 1000=2 to the power of 3=8. To convert decimal numbers to binary, divide throughout by 2. Whenever there is a remainder, record it as 1. If there is no remainder, write down 0. Write down the numbers from right to left. For example, suppose we want to convert 27 into binary. We put it down like this:

2)27					
2)13 rem. 1	write 1 in column A				
2) 6 rem. 1	write 1 in column B	E	D	C	B	A
2) 3 rem. 0	write 0 in column C				
2) 1 rem. 1	write 1 in column D				
0 rem. 1	write 1 in column E	1	1	0	1	1
	Answer:				
	27=11011				

To convert a binary number to decimal, first of all write down the binary number and under each figure, starting from the right, write down the powers of 2 in consecutive order until every figure has a power of 2 written beneath it. Let us take the binary number, 101011, as an example.

$$1 \quad 0 \quad 1 \quad 0 \quad 1 \quad 1$$
$$2^5 \quad 2^4 \quad 2^3 \quad 2^2 \quad 2^1 \quad 2^0$$

Now, calculate every power of 2 which has a 1 above it and write it down. Thus:

$$2^5 = 2 \times 2 \times 2 \times 2 \times 2 = 32$$
$$2^3 = 2 \times 2 \times 2 = 8$$
$$2^1 = 2 = 2$$
$$2^0 = 1 = 1$$

Add the answers together: $\overline{43}$

Therefore binary 101011 = 43 in the decimal system.

The advantage of the binary system lies in its use for computers. Electrical switches can have essentially only two positions, "on" and "off". Computers, which are made of thousands of individual electronic switches, need the binary system. If the state of series of these switches is controlled, many hundreds of numbers can be "memorised" and recognised by the computer as a series of 1's or 0's.

World Calendars

The Roman Calendar
The Romans used a calendar that dated from the foundation of Rome (753 B.C. according to our own calendar reckoning). Their year was 304 days long, divided into ten months, beginning with March. Later, the months of January and February were added, making a total of 355 days in the year. About 700 years after the foundation of Rome, Julius Caesar discovered that the calendar had fallen into confusion. With the help of an Egyptian astronomer, he redesigned the calendar so that the year became 365 days long, with an extra day every fourth year (the Leap Year). The Julian Calendar, as it came to be known, is the one on which our own calendar is based.

The Gregorian Calendar
Sometime around the sixth century A.D., the numbering of the years was changed to start with the birth of Christ, and each year was signified by the letters A.D. or *Anno Domini* (in the year of Our Lord). The letters B.C. (Before Christ) denote the years before the birth of Jesus and are counted backwards. Thus, 300 B.C. is *earlier* than 200 B.C., while 300 A.D. is *later* than 200 A.D. In other respects, the Christian Calendar was the same as the Julian Calendar. However, in 1582, it was found that making *every* fourth year a Leap Year had resulted in a discrepancy of about ten days. Pope Gregory decided to lose the extra ten days and ordained that October 5, 1582, should be called October 15, and that in future only one in four of the end-of-century years should be Leap Years. In this way, neither 1800 nor 1900 were Leap Years but the year 2000 will be. The Gregorian Calendar was gradually adopted by the countries of the world over the next 400 years. The changeover was made in England in 1752, when Wednesday, September 2, 1752, was followed by Thursday, September 14.

The Jewish Calendar
The starting point of the Jewish Calendar corresponds to October 7, 3761 B.C. It is based on the Jewish belief that the Era of Creation occurred at the time of the Autumnal Equinox in 3760 B.C. The normal calendar year of the Jews is divided into 12 months and lasts only 354 days, but so that there shall not be too great a difference from the solar year, a thirteenth month is occasionally added to the Jewish year.

The Moslem Calendar
The Moslem Calendar starts with the *Hejira*, or the flight of Muhammad from Mecca to Medina, which corresponds to July 16, A.D. 622.

The Ancient Greek Calendar
The Ancient Greeks reckoned their time in *Olympiads*, which were

cycles of four years corresponding to the Olympic Games held on the plain of Olympia every fourth year. Each Olympiad was given the name of the victor at games. The first Olympiad we know about is that of Choroebus, 776 B.C.

Leap Years

The length of a year corresponds to a solar year, or the time the Earth takes to go round the Sun. However, the average solar year is 365.242 days and the seasons would eventually be thrown into confusion if the extra quarter of a day were not taken into account. To maintain a proper balance, therefore, every fourth year contains one extra day, making 366 in all. The extra day is February 29. It occurs in those years that are divisible by four: for example, 1964, 1968, 1972, etc. But there is yet one more complication concerned with Leap Years. The solar year is in fact not quite $365\frac{1}{4}$ days long and this means making another small adjustment. Consequently, centennial years (1300, 1700, 1900, etc) are treated as ordinary years unless the first two figures of the year are divisible by four. 1200 and 1600 were leap years, 2000 will be one too, because 12, 16 and 20 are all divisible by four.

The Seasons

In the Northern Hemisphere, the four seasons are:
Spring from the Vernal Equinox (about March 21) to the Summer Solstice (June 21).
Summer from the Summer Solstice to the Autumnal Equinox (about September 21).
Autumn from the Autumnal Equinox to the Winter Solstice (about December 21).
Winter from the Winter Solstice to the Vernal Equinox. In the Southern Hemisphere, the seasons are reversed. Spring corresponding to Autumn, Summer to Winter, Autumn to Spring and Winter to Summer. We think of Christmas Day as falling in mid-Winter and are delighted if snow falls and we get a white Christmas. But if you lived in Australia, you would celebrate Christmas in the summertime and eat your turkey in the sunshine.

The Solstices are the two days of the year when the Sun is furthest from the Equator. The Summer Solstice, therefore, in the Northern Hemisphere is the longest day (in terms of daylight), the Winter Solstice the shortest day.

The Equinoxes occur when the Sun crosses the Equator and day and night are of equal length.

Easter Day Unlike Christmas Day, which is always December 25, Easter Day is a moveable feast. According to English Law, it is calculated as the first Sunday following the first full moon after the Vernal (or spring) Equinox. Many people would like Easter to become a fixed feast, and in 1928, Parliament passed the Easter Act, which would have fixed Easter Day as "the first Sunday after the second Saturday in April". However, the Act required the support of the various international Churches and this was not given. So, for the time being at any rate, Easter remains a moveable feast.

The Months of the Year

Name	Named after	Length in days
January	Janus, Roman god of the portal, who faces two ways, the past and future.	31
February	Februa, Roman Festival of Purification.	28 (29 in Leap Year)
March	Mars, Roman god of war (originally the 1st month).	31
April	Aperire, Latin verb "to open"; when the earth opens to receive seed.	30
May	Maia, Roman goddess of growth and increase.	31
June	Junius, from the Latin "gens", meaning family	30
July	Julius Caesar. At one time, the month was called Quintilis or 5th month.	31
August	Julius Caesar Augustus. Formerly Sextilis or 6th month.	31
September	Septem, meaning seven, or 7th month.	30
October	Octo, eight, or 8th month.	31
November	Novem, nine, or 9th month.	30
December	Decem, ten, or 10th month.	31

The Days of the Week

Name	Named after
Monday	Moon's Day
Tuesday	Tiu's Day. Tiu is the Anglo-Saxon counterpart of Tyr, the Nordic god of war, and son of Odin.
Wednesday	Woden, Anglo-Saxon for Odin, Nordic messenger of victory.
Thursday	Thor, Nordic god of thunder, eldest son of Odin.
Friday	Frigg's Day. Frigg or Freyja was the wife of Odin and Nordic goddess of love.
Saturday	Saturn's Day
Sunday	Sun's Day

Greenwich Mean Time

Time in the British Isles is known as *Greenwich Mean Time*. During the summer months, however, *British Summer Time* operates, when the clocks are one hour ahead of G.M.T. This gives us one hour's extra daylight in the evenings, reducing by one hour the amount of daylight before we get up in the morning. B.S.T. is in force usually from March to October and throughout this period our time is the same as the Continent's. From 1968 to 1971, *British Standard Time* operated, which meant that our clocks were one hour ahead of G.M.T. throughout the year. Public outcry, however, forced the Government to return to G.M.T. in October, 1971.

Standard Time

In 1883, *International Time Zones* were established. The world is now divided into 24 time zones or segments, each measuring 15° of longitude. The 12 zones to the west of Britain are behind Greenwich Mean Time, while the 12 zones to the east are in front of G.M.T. To avoid confusion, however, most countries have established a standard time which applies throughout the country. The standard time is loosely based on the international time zones. Some countries which are very large (like the United States) have more than one standard time. The table below shows the time in some of the major cities of the world when it is 1200 hours G.M.T., or 1300 hours B.S.T. in London.

Adelaide, Australia	2130 hours
Aden	1500 hours
Algiers, Algeria	1400 hours
Amsterdam, Holland	1300 hours
Antwerp, Belgium	1300 hours
Athens, Greece	1400 hours
Auckland, New Zealand	2400 hours
Baltimore, U.S.A.	0700 hours
Berlin	1300 hours
Bermuda	0900 hours
Bombay, India	1730 hours
Borneo	2000 hours
Boston, U.S.A.	0700 hours
Brisbane, Australia	2200 hours
Buenos Aires, Argentina	0800 hours
Cairo, Egypt	1400 hours
Calcutta, India	1800 hours
Cape Town, South Africa	1400 hours
Chicago, U.S.A,	0600 hours
Copenhagen, Denmark	1300 hours
Hong Kong	2000 hours
Honolulu	0200 hours
Leningrad, U.S.S.R.	1500 hours
Lima, Peru	0700 hours
Mecca	1440 hours
Melbourne, Australia	2200 hours
Mexico City, Mexico	0500 hours
Montreal, Canada	0700 hours
New Orleans, U.S.A.	0600 hours
New York, U.S.A.	0700 hours

Odessa, U.S.S.R.	1500 hours
Perth, Western Australia	2000 hours
Paris, France	1300 hours
Rangoon, Burma	1830 hours
San Francisco, U.S.A.	0400 hours
Singapore	1930 hours
Stockholm, Sweden	1300 hours
Sydney, Australia	2200 hours
Tokyo, Japan	2100 hours
Vancouver, Canada	0400 hours
Wellington, New Zealand	2400 hours
Zanzibar	1500 hours

The International Date Line, or line where the change of date occurs, runs down the 180th meridian, or 180° longitude, with a few variations for geographical or political reasons.

Watches at Sea
The 24 hours of the day are divided at sea into watches, each four hours long except for the period between 1600 hours and 2000 hours which is split into two two-hour dog watches. The watches are known as follows:

2400 to 0400 hours	Middle Watch
0400 to 0800 hours	Morning Watch
0800 to 1200 hours	Forenoon Watch
1200 to 1600 hours	Afternoon Watch
1600 to 1800 hours	First Dog Watch
1800 to 2000 hours	Second Dog Watch
2000 to 2400 hours	First Watch

In the Home
Cookery

British Measures
$\frac{1}{8}$ pint = $\frac{1}{2}$ gill = 4 tablespoons = $\frac{1}{4}$ cup British Standard Measure = 71 ml.

$\frac{1}{4}$ pint = 1 gill = 8 tablespoons = $\frac{1}{2}$ cup British Standard
Measure = 142 ml.
1 pint = 2 cups British Standard Measure = 0.568 litre
1 quart = 2 pints = 4 cups British Standard Measure = 1.14 litres
1 gallon = 4 quarts = 8 pints = 16 cups British Standard Measure = 4.5 litres

American Measures
1 American pint = 16 fluid oz. = 0.454 litre
1 British pint = 20 fluid oz. = 0.568 litre
1 American cup measure = 8 fluid oz. = 227 ml.
1 American tablespoon = 3 flat teaspoons
(All American spoon measures are a flat spoonful)
1 American cup of flour = $4\frac{1}{2}$ oz. = 127 g.
1 American cup of sugar = 7 oz. = 198 g.
1 American cup of butter = 7 oz. = 198 g.
1 American tablespoon of flour = $\frac{1}{2}$ oz. = 14 g.
1 American tablespoon of sugar = $\frac{3}{4}$ oz. = 21 g.
1 American tablespoon of butter = $\frac{3}{4}$ oz. = 21 g.

Handy British Measures

Flour	1 level cup = just over 5 oz. = 143 g.
	$1\frac{1}{2}$ level cups = about $\frac{1}{2}$ lb. = 227 g.
	$\frac{3}{4}$ level cup = about $\frac{1}{4}$ lb. = 113 g.
Sugar	1 level cup castor or gran. sugar = $\frac{1}{2}$ lb. = 227 g.
	1 level cup demerara sugar = 7 oz. = 198 g.
	1 level cup sifted icing sugar = 5 oz. = 142 g.
Dried fruit varies according to the fruit. Average is	1 level cup = 6 oz. = 170 g.
Syrup or treacle	1 level cup = 1 lb. = 454 g.
Jam	1 level cup = $\frac{3}{4}$ to 1 lb. = 340-454 g.
Fresh breadcrumbs	1 level cup = 5 oz. = 142 g.
Fat	1 level cup = $\frac{1}{2}$ lb. = 227 g.

Oven Temperatures

	Temperature	Regulo	Main Setting
Very slow	240°—280°F	$\frac{1}{4}$—$\frac{1}{2}$	A—B
Slow	280°—320°F	1	C
Warm	320°—340°F	3	C
Moderate	340°—370°F	4	D
Fairly hot	370°—400°F	5—6	E
Hot	400°—440°F	7	F
Very hot	440°—480°F	8—9	G—H

Cookery Terms

Aspic	Savoury jelly
Au gras	Cooked with meat or meat stock
Au gratin	Method of cooking which gives a brown

	surface, often of grated cheese
Bain-marie	Pan of water in which smaller dishes can be cooked at a slow temperature
Beurre Manié	Butter and flour worked together into a paste
Bouchées	Small cases of puff pastry
Bouquet garni	Muslin bags of herbs, usually parsley, thyme and bayleaf, used for flavouring stews, etc.
Court bouillon	Liquid used for cooking fish
Croquettes	Cone-shaped balls of minced meat, fish or potatoes, egg-and-breadcrumbed and fried
Croûtons	Fried or toasted bread, cut in pieces and served with soup
Demi-glace	Brown sauce, semi-clear and syrupy
Escalope	Thin slice of meat, usually veal
Flan	Open tart, cooked in a ring
Frappé	Iced
Hors-d'oeuvre	Dish of small tasty morsels served at the start of the meal
Macédoine	Vegetables or fruit cut in even-sized pieces
Marinade	Liquid containing herbs and seasoning in which meat, fish or vegetables are soaked before cooking
Mask	To coat with sauce
Mornay	With a cheese sauce
Mousse	Light savoury or sweet mixture
Navarin	A stew of lamb or mutton
Noisettes	Small rounds of meat taken from lamb or mutton cutlets
Panade	Paste of flour, butter, and a little liquid
Pâté	Savoury mixture of finely-minced liver
Pot-au-feu	Beef boiled with vegetables and the stock thus obtained used for soup
Praline	Flavoured with almond rock
Purée	Pulp of vegetables or fruit put through a sieve
Ragoût	A stew
Roux	Mixture of melted fat and flour, which forms the basis of many sauces
Sauté	Fried in shallow fat
Tournedos	Fillet of beef
Tutti-frutti	Mixture of fruits
Vinaigrette	Mixture of oil, vinegar and seasonings
Vol-au-vent	Case of puff pastry
Zest	Thin coloured skin of orange or lemon used to give flavour, removed without

taking the bitter white pith; the oil extracted from orange or lemon skins

Dressmaking

Most paper patterns these days give very clear directions on how to make up the garment. Stock sizes may vary according to the manufacturer, but the envelope in which the paper pattern is contained will give the sizes on which that particular garment is based. When buying dress material, always find out from the assistant the width of the fabric: as a rule, the thinner fabrics, cotton, silk, rayons, etc., are 90 cm. wide; thicker fabrics, woollens, tweeds, etc., are 115 cm. or 140 cm. in width. While buying the material, it is a good idea to buy the notions you will need at the same time—that is, the sewing thread, seam binding, zip fastener, ribbon, etc.—so that you can be sure of getting the right colour. Before you actually cut the material, read the pattern instructions carefully and study the diagrams which show how the pieces should be pinned to fabric. Shorten or lengthen the pattern, if necessary, before cutting out.

Most pattern manufacturers use similar symbols on their patterns. There may be some variations, but the following examples will show you what to expect:

Grain line, indicating straight threads, either lengthwise or crosswise. The pattern should be placed on the fabric so that the grain line is parallel with the long or cross threads.

Broken line indicates the stitching line.

Notches indicate matching points for joining seams. The seams to be joined will have the same number of notches.

Darts are usually folded along the solid line, stitched along the broken line.

Circular marks should be indicated on the material with either tailors' chalk or tailors' tacks. Tailors' tacks are made with contrasting-coloured thread, which is stitched twice through both pattern and fabric, leaving generous loops on either side. Before removing the pattern, cut the loops, which then show where a dart or pleat is to be made.

Taking your measurements

Bust	Measure round the bust, keeping the tape-measure well up at the back.
Waist	Measure round the natural waist-line.

Taking Your Measurements

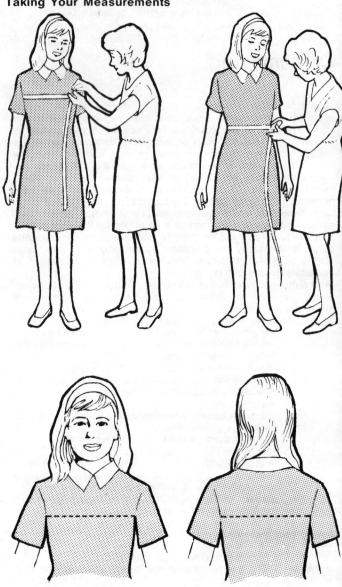

Hips	First measure round the widest part of the hips: that is, about twenty cm. below the waist. Then measure round the point of the hip-bones, about seven to ten cm. below the waist.
Shoulder to waist	Place the tape-measure at the top of the collar-bone, near the neck, and measure over the bust to the waist.
Shoulder to hemline	Follow the same directions as before but carry the tape-measure down to the hemline.
Shoulder waist (back)	Place the tape-measure at the top of the shoulder, near the neck, and measure over the shoulder blades to waist.
Shoulder to hemline (back)	Follow the same directions, carrying the tape measure to the hemline.
Across the chest	Measure across the chest, from armhole to armhole, just above the bust and below the base of the throat.
Across the back	Measure across the back from armhole to armhole.
Sleeve— back length	With bent arm, measure from five cm. below the shoulder at the armhole, over the elbow to 2.5 cm beyond the wrist bone.
Sleeve— inside length	With the arm straight, measure from the armpit to the inside of the wrist.
Wrist	Measure round wrist.
Elbow	Flex the arm, and measure round elbow and forearm.
Upper arm	With the arm relaxed, measure round the thickest part of the arm above the elbow.
Hemline	Take approximate measurements from waist to just above the knee (or wherever you like the length of your skirt to be). When pinning up the hem, ask someone to adjust it for you and to check that it is level. This will be easier for them if you stand on a chair.

Knitting

Casting on
There are two methods of casting on. One uses two needles and i

probably the easiest to manage if you are a beginner. The other uses one needle and your thumb.

Method I Make a slip-knot and place the loop on the left-hand needle. Holding the wool in the right hand, put the point of the second needle into the loop *(fig. 1)*. Wind the wool round the point of the right-hand needle, from back to front, and draw it through, thus forming a second loop *(fig. 2)*. Slip this loop on to the left-hand needle *(fig. 3)*, and repeat the process until you have the desired number of stitches.

Method II This is usually preferred by the expert knitter as it gives a neater edge. First, draw off, say, a yard of wool and wind it once round your thumb. Place the point of the needle through the loop round your thumb *(fig. 4)*. With the wool connected to the main ball, wind it round the needle and draw it through. Gently pull taut the stitch formed. Using the yard length of wool, make another loop

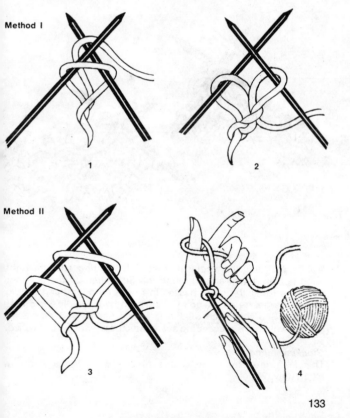

Method I

1

2

Method II

3

4

round your thumb and repeat the process. The stitches form on the needle as you go along. The main difficulty about this method is estimating how much wool to draw off in the first place. Nothing is worse than having to undo 60 or 70 stitches because you have left yourself insufficient wool to cast on 90. It is better to allow too much.

Plain knitting (Fig. 5)
Stick the right-hand needle upwards through the first stitch on the left-hand needle, so that the point passes behind the left-hand needle. Wrap the wool, held in the right hand, round the point of the right-hand needle and draw it through. Slip the first stitch off the left-hand needle and continue the whole process with the next stitch. Repeat until all the stitches on the left-hand needle have been worked and transferred to the right-hand needle. You will then have completed one row.

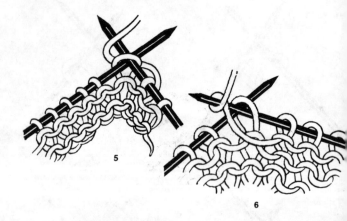

Purl knitting (Fig. 6)
Making sure that the wool is in front of the knitting, stick the right-hand needle downwards through the first stitch on the left-hand needle, so that the point passes in front of the left-hand needle. Wrap the wool round the point of the right-hand needle and draw it through. Slip the stitch off the left-hand needle and repeat the process with each succeeding stitch until the whole row is finished.

Stocking stitch (Fig. 7)
This is formed by working one plain row and one purl row alternately.

134

Increasing (Fig. 8)

Knit the stitch in the usual way, but before slipping it off the left-hand needle, stick the point of the right-hand needle through the back of the same stitch and knit it again. Then slip the stitch off the left-hand needle.

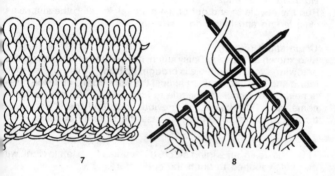

7

8

Decreasing (Fig. 9)

Knit two stitches together.

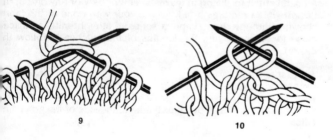

9

10

Casting-off (Fig. 10)

Knit two stitches. Using the point of the left-hand needle, draw the right-hand stitch over the second stitch knitted, leaving one stitch on the right-hand needle. Knit another stitch and repeat the process, till only one stitch is left. Break off the wool and draw the end through the last stitch. Pull taut.

Needlework

Running stitch (Figs. 1 and 2)
Run the needle in and out of the material, keeping the stitches at even length and following a straight line.

Chain stitch (Fig. 3)
Also known as the Lazy Daisy stitch. It is always worked downwards or towards you. The needle is brought up from the wrong side of the fabric and inserted again at almost the same point, while the thread is held down under the needle to form a loop. The needle should come up a little below the previous loop and the thread pulled through, but not too tightly in case the material puckers.

Blanket stitch (Fig. 4)
This is basically an edging stitch. It is worked from left to right, with one stitch looped through the one before.

Cross stitch (Fig. 5)
Two straight stitches of equal length are placed across each other at right angles to form a cross and the crosses are worked in a line to form a border pattern.

Satin stitch (Fig. 6)
A useful stitch for filling in leaves in embroidery or any part of the design which requires a flat, even colour with none of the fabric showing through. It is simply a series of straight stitches placed close together, varying the lengths of the stitches to follow the design.

Stem stitch (Fig. 7)
An outline stitch used in embroidery for the stems of plants and veins of leaves. It is worked from the bottom upwards, each stitch being placed so that it overlaps a little to the side of the preceding stitch.

French knot
Bring the needle up from the wrong side and take up a small piece of material as though you were going to make a simple stitch. Before pulling the thread through, however, wind it once, twice or three times round the needle to form a knot. Hold the knot down, pull the thread taut and fasten it down by pushing the needle through to the back of the material before either fastening off or proceeding to the next knot.

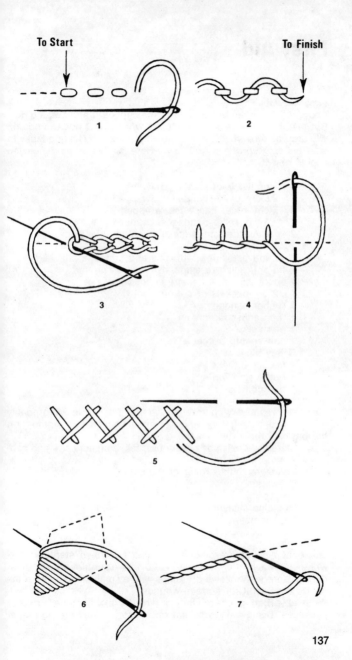

First Aid

First Aid Kit

Your mother no doubt has a medicine cupboard and first aid box. But just in case an emergency arises when she is not around and you are not sure what her first aid kit contains, it is a good idea to start building up one of your own. Here is a list of the things you should aim to collect:

> 4 triangular bandages in envelopes
> 3×2.5-cm. roller bandages, wrapped
> 3×5-cm. roller bandages, wrapped
> 2×7.5-cm. roller bandages, wrapped
> 9 First Aid dressings (small, medium, and large)
> 2×25 g. packets of lint
> 6 wound dressings, with pad and bandage attached
> 1 tin adhesive dressings, assorted sizes
> 1 spool 2.5 cm. $\times$ 1 metre adhesive plaster
> 4×25 g. packets of cotton wool
> 1 rubber bandage
> 1 tube antiseptic cream
> 1 pair scissors
> 1 pair splinter forceps
> Safety pins, assorted
> 1 medicine measure
> 1 bottle smelling salts
> 1 thermometer

This list gives a very comprehensive first aid kit and will probably take some time to get together. Essential items which should form the basis of the kit would be:

> Sterilised dressings of various sizes, both adhesive and non-adhesive
> Bandages, either roller or triangular
> Scissors
> Forceps
> Medicine measure
> Thermometer

Dressings

The best type of dressing is one that has been sterilised and wrapped in a protective covering so that no infection can enter during storage. Adhesive dressings with a small strip of lint in the centre are useful for surface wounds.

White absorbent gauze or white or pink lint is obtainable in rolls or packages. Disadvantage is that once opened they are no longer completely sterile. Care should be taken to rewrap them quickly once a piece has been cut off.

Bandages
Different sized roller bandages should be used as follows: finger—2.5 cm. width; arm and hand—5 to 7.5 cm. in width; leg—10 cm. Triangular bandages are made by cutting diagonally in half a piece of cotton or linen measuring about 96 cm. square. The diagrams below show how they should be folded. They are also useful as slings for supporting the arm or shoulder.

Triangular bandage

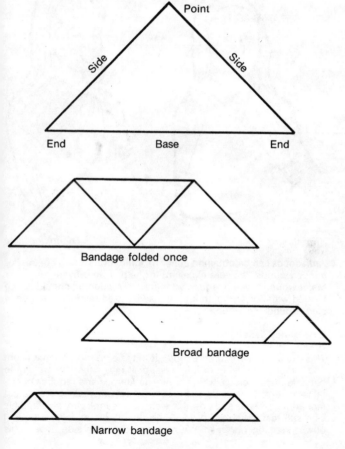

Bandage folded once

Broad bandage

Narrow bandage

Roller bandage

Head

Free end

Arm sling

Triangular sling

Antiseptics can be obtained either in liquid form or as a cream. For minor wounds, they are excellent for helping to prevent infection. Major wounds, which require attention from a doctor, should not be treated with antiseptic, though it may be used to clean the area of skin around the wound.

Emergency Treatment
Shock
This occurs in all injured people. It may be no more than a slight and temporary feeling of faintness, or it may cause the patient to become unconscious, which is very dangerous and requires hospital treatment. Shock acts on the nervous system, making the patient feel faint and cold and possibly sick. He will look very pale and his skin will feel clammy. To deal with the condition, lay the patient down, keeping his head low and turned to one side, loosen his

clothing and wrap him in a blanket or rug. Give him some water or warm tea if he complains of thirst. If, in spite of this, the patient grows worse, call an ambulance immediately.

Bruising
Pressure and cold water are the best forms of treatment for a bruise. For a blow on the eye, a rolled handkerchief tied tightly with a bandage may stop the blow developing into a black eye.

Jagged wounds
Use pressure to stop the bleeding. Treat with an antiseptic, place a clean dressing over the wound, cover with a pad of cotton wool and bandage firmly with a roller bandage.

Clean-cut wounds
Press the edges of the wound together, apply a clean dressing and a pad of cotton wool and bandage firmly.

Abrasions
Most common in children, usually caused by a fall on gravel. The abrasion should be thoroughly cleaned with soap and warm water so that all the gravel and dirt are washed away. Cover with plenty of antiseptic cream and a clean dressing and pad, and bandage.

Nose-bleed
Caused by the rupture of a small blood vessel in the front part of the nose. Make the patient lean forward slightly and press the soft part of his nose between your finger and thumb. He may feel slightly uncomfortable but after a few minutes a clot will form and the bleeding will stop.

Splinters, etc.
Do not attempt to remove the splinter unless a large part projects from the skin. Cover with a dressing and take the patient to the doctor, especially if the splinter is of metal or glass.

Burns and scalds
Blisters formed by minor burns and scalds should not be pricked because this will increase the risk of infection. Cover the area with antiseptic cream and a small dressing and bandage firmly with a roller bandage. Major burns and scalds should be quickly covered with sterile dressings, bandaged in position, and an ambulance called as soon as possible.

Sprains
Cold water applied to the swollen joint will help to ease the pain and reduce the swelling. If bandages are available, bind the joint up, first soaking the bandage in cold water.

Foreign body in the eye

Pull down the lower lid to see if the foreign body, usually a bit of grit, is there. If it is, draw the corner of a clean handkerchief across the speck to remove it. If the speck is on the eyball, close the lid, place a pad of cotton wool over the eye, bandage it in position and take the patient for medical treatment.

Fainting

Fainting is caused by a weakened action of the heart which lowers the blood pressure and gives an insufficient supply of blood to the brain. Lay the patient down, loosen the clothing at the neck, chest and waist and lower the patient's head so that the blood reaches the brain more easily. See that there is plenty of fresh air. Smelling salts will help the patient to recover consciousness. A cup of tea may only be given after the patient is completely conscious again.

Cramp

Continuous massage should relieve this very painful condition.

Dog bites and cat bites

The danger of infection is very great because the wounds are narrow and usually deep and not easily cleaned. Cover the area with a sterile dressing and send the patient to the doctor.

Insect bites

Bee-stings and wasp-stings may give the patient shock. Remove the sting, if present, with a needle, which has been sterilised in the flame of a match and apply a solution of baking soda and water. Keep the patient calm.

Artificial respiration

There are three methods of getting a patient to breathe: *The Schäfer method*—lay the patient on his stomach, with the head turned to one side. Kneel by his hips, placing your hands over the patient's lower ribs with the wrists almost touching and the thumbs as close as possible. The fingers should be round the patient's sides. Sway forwards and backwards about 12 times a minute, keeping the arms straight. Continue until the patient is breathing normally.
The Holger Nielsen method—lay the patient face downwards with his arms bent forwards and his forehead resting on his hands. Kneel on one knee in line with the patient's head and place the other foot by the patient's elbow. Put your hands on his back over the shoulder blades with the fingers pointing towards his feet. Sway forward with straight arms, counting one second, two seconds. This applies pressure to the patient's back and forces the air out of his lungs. Now, draw your hands back over his shoulders, down the upper arms to just above the elbows. Raise the patient's arms without lifting his body off the ground. Count one second, two

seconds. Lower his arms and put your hands on the patient's back again, ready to repeat the first movement. The two exercises should be carried out ten times a minute until the patient begins to breathe.

Schäfer method

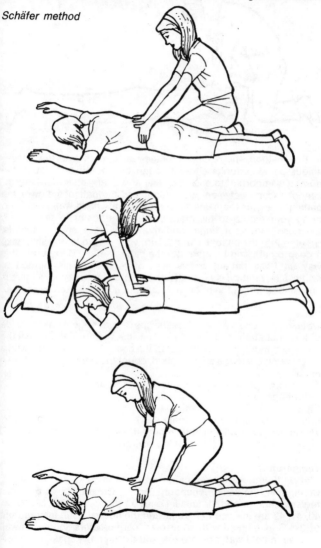

Holger Nielsen method

Kiss of life

In this method, the rescuer breathes air directly into the unconscious person's lungs either through the mouth or through the nose. It is important to ensure a clear airway and make sure that air cannot escape between your mouth and the patient's. Lower the patient's jaw, at the same time pressing his head well back, and bring your mouth to his mouth, making a complete seal. Pinch the nose with your finger and thumb to close off the nostrils. Breathe into the patient's lungs. Turn your mouth to one side, take a deep breath and breathe into the patient again. Carry on in this way until the patient shows sign of recovery. This method of artificial respiration is most effective with children because there is no risk of injuring them through too much pressure on their ribs.

Pulse

To take someone's pulse, place the tips of your fingers on the inside of his wrist about half an inch in from the thumb. You will feel the artery expanding with each beat of the heart. Timing yourself with a wrist-watch bearing a second hand, count the number of beats in a minute.

The normal pulse rate varies according to age.

Grown-ups: 60-90 beats a minute.

Children: 90-100 beats a minute.

Infants: 100-140 beats a minute.

The pulse rate will be slightly higher if the patient is standing or if he is excited or has been taking exercise.

Temperature

Clinical thermometers normally register from 35° Centigrade to 42° Centigrade, the scale commonly used in Britain. The larger lines register degrees and the smaller ones 0.1 of a degree; 35, 36, 38, 39, 40, 41, 42 are marked in figures, and the normal adult temperature of 37° C. is marked with an arrow. Thermometers should be well washed in cold water before use and the mercury shaken down. A temperature is usually taken under the tongue, allowing two minutes, or it can be taken by placing the thermometer under the armpit or in the groin.

Etiquette

Etiquette is mainly a matter of simple courtesy, and most rules of etiquette are basically showing consideration for other people. These days the rules are far fewer than they used to be, which is a good thing because life is freer and more friendly than it was in Victorian days. Nevertheless, the rules that remain are important and should be remembered.

Visiting
When you intend to call on someone, try to write or telephone first to find out the most convenient time. It is perfectly all right, however, to call without warning if you are enquiring after the health of someone who is ill, but do not expect to be asked in.

Introductions
Younger people should be introduced to older people and men should be introduced to women. Easiest method is to say simply, "May I introduce my friend, Jane. She and I are in the same form," or words to that effect. It always helps if you can give some brief information about the person you are introducing, especially at parties when you may have to leave people together when the introductions are over.

Travelling
On a crowded bus or train, always give up your seat to an older person. It is wrong to think that you "have paid for your seat"—as you sometimes hear people say. You have paid simply to travel in the bus or train and seats are merely provided for greater comfort. Those who are standing have paid for their tickets just as you have and it is common courtesy to allow an older person to sit down.

Thank-you letters
These should be written without delay, whether they are for a

present or for a pleasant afternoon out. Do not spend too long worrying about what to say—it is better to write a short thank-you letter promptly than to leave it so long that you are too embarrassed to write at all. After an informal tea-party it is quite correct to telephone your thanks.

Breeds of Horses

American Quarter Horse   Originally bred in Virginia, U.S.A., to race along quarter-mile tracks cut out of the wilderness. Most American Quarter Horses can trace their ancestry from Janus, an English Thoroughbred who flourished in Virginia between 1756 and 1780. They stand about 15 h.h. and have great speed from 180 metres to 400 metres, which is their limit. They are excellent for cattle work, having great strength and nimbleness.

American Saddle Horse   Height is 15 to 16 hands, appearance light and elegant with high head and tail carriage. Today, it is usually bred for the show-ring.

Andalusian   Sure-footed Spanish horse of good temperament and a strong body.

Anglo-Arab   A cross between the Arab and the Thoroughbred, which may show characteristics of either. It makes a good dressage horse and, with the stamina and intelligence of the Arab, is a fine hunter and hack.

Appaloosa   Distinguished by its spotted appearance (black or chocolate spots on a white coat), it measures 14.2 to 15.2 h.h. and makes an excellent riding horse. Its name is derived from a breed developed by the Nez Percé Indians in the Palouse country of Central Idaho and Eastern Washington.

Arab   Probably the most beautiful horse in the world, it is also the oldest breed. Its outstanding characteristics are its smallness (about 14.2 to 15 hands), the concave profile of its head and its extremely graceful head and tail carriage.

Cleveland Bay   The breed is indigenous to Northern England. Standing 15.3 to 16 h.h. it has always been famous as a carriage horse but it is also strong enough to be used for farmwork. It is popular for crossing with a Thoroughbred to obtain a strong hunter with stamina and good conformation.

Clydesdale   Heavy horse with a flat, broad head and good feet and

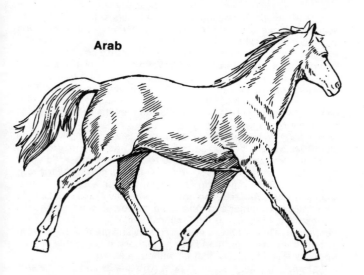

Arab

limbs, it dates from the mid-18th century when Flemish stallions were imported to produce greater weight in the native Lanarkshire breed. It is used for haulage work and agriculture.

Cob Short-legged riding horse or pony with an arched neck, short back and wide girth. Its equable temperament makes it a popular hack, with the advantage that it is capable of carrying plenty of weight.

Connemara Irish pony measuring 13 to 14 hands with a well-balanced head and neck and free action. It is a tough, wiry breed, which does well on poor keep.

Dales Strong native pony from the east of the Pennines. It stands up to 14.2 hands and is extremely hardy.

Dartmoor Attractive, good-natured pony that is tough and long lived. Though no bigger than 12.2 hands, it is up to a great amount of weight and will carry an adult happily and comfortably.

Exmoor Another attractive, tough little pony, very suitable for children and in harness. Height, 12.3 hands maximum. It is characterized by its mealy muzzle.

Fell Strong pony, formerly used as a pack pony, which comes from the west of the Pennines. Good for both riding and driving. Average height is 13.2 hands.

Hackney Harness-horse with a characteristic high-stepping, exaggerated action. Height ranges from 14.3 to 15.3 hands. Head and tail are carried high: nowadays, Hackney horses and ponies are bred almost exclusively for the show-ring.

Highland The largest and strongest of British mountain and moorland breeds, it measures up to 14.2 hands. It is usually very docile and has always been used for carrying stalkers in the Highlands. It is extremely sure-footed.

Morgan American light horse, descended from a little bay stallion, Justin Morgan, which was foaled in Vermont in 1793. It is a solidly-built, muscular horse, varying between 14 and 15 h.h.

Mustang American saddle-horse and cow-pony, descended from horses introduced into America by the Spaniards in the 16th century. Generally speaking, the Mustang is little to look at but is extremely courageous and hardy.

New Forest When properly broken-in, it is a particularly suitable mount for a child, because it has grown so accustomed to roads and traffic while roaming the 24,000 hectares of the New Forest. It measures 12 to 14.2 h.h. and is very sure-footed, docile and friendly.

Palomino Strictly speaking, not a breed but a colour. Found mainly in North America, the horse is generally Arabian or Barb in appearance but larger and more solid. Its colour is golden and the mane and tail should be light, almost white.

Percheron Draught horse with short legs and great strength. With a short body, deep girth and heavy quarters, it is capable of hard work. Its legs are clean, that is, without feathers.

Polo Pony Any neat, compact pony with quality and stamina and, above all, nimbleness and speed. Its looks are immaterial as long as its performance is good. The most famous polo pony in fiction was Rudyard Kipling's The Maltese Cat who was described as the "Past Pluperfect Prestissimo Player of Polo."

Shetland Small but strong pony, measuring not more than 10

Shetland

hands. It is very appealing to look at, with its thick mane and tail and well-proportioned body. It is docile and lovable and popular with children.

Shire The greatest of the heavy horses, standing over 17 hands, and immensely strong. Its forbears were the great horses of England, used as war-horses and having to carry men in armour weighing as much as 190 kilos. It has an arched neck, lean head, deep body and a considerable amount of feather on the legs.

Suffolk Punch Clean-legged draught horse that is always chestnut in colour. It stands about 16 hands and is very wide both in front and in the quarters.

Welsh Mountain Probably the prettiest of Britain's native ponies, with a small neat head, little, close-set pointed ears, large eyes and a gay tail carriage. Small and strong (about 12.2 h.h.), it is very popular as a mount for children.

Breeds of Dogs

Breed	First brought to Britain	Purpose or origin
Afghan Hound	1894	Native hound of Afghanistan
Airedale Terrier	1850s—cross between Otterhound and terrier	Keeping down vermin along river banks
Alsatian	1920s	Originally German shepherd dogs: in Britain used by Police, Services and as guide dogs
Australian Cattle Dog	—	Cattle-droving
Basenji	1936	Hunting antelope in the Congo

Breed	First brought to Britain	Purpose or origin
Basset Hound	1866	Originated in Artois, France
Beagle	Before 16th century	Hunting hares
Bedlington Terrier	Developed in Northumberland, late 18th century	Sporting terrier
Bloodhound	Introduced by William the Conqueror	Tracking dog, once used for hunting deer
Border Terrier	Early breed, common in Northern England	Sporting dog
Borzoi	1875	Wolf-hunting in Russia
Boston Terrier	1875	American cross between English/ French bulldogs
Boxer	1911	Bull-fighting in Germany
Bull Terrier	Created 19th century	Sporting dog
Bulldog	Indigenous	Bull-baiting
Bull Mastiff	1924	Guard dog
Cairn Terrier	Developed in Hebrides	Routing out foxes, etc.
Chihuahua	20th century	Descended from sacred dogs of the Aztecs
Chow Chow	1789	Chinese. Bred for its fur
Clumber Spaniel	Developed about 1770	Retrieving
Cocker Spaniel	1860s	Retrieving
Collie (Rough)	Indigenous	Sheep-herding
Collie (Smooth)	1860s	Sheep-herding
Dachshund	19th century	Badger-digging in Germany
Dalmatian	18th century	Guards for mail coaches
Dandie Dinmont Terrier	Older Border breed	Sporting dog
Deerhound	Ancient British breed	Deer-coursing
Dingo	—	Native dog of Australia
Dobermann	20th century	Guard dog
Elkhound	1870s	Bird-, elk- or

Great Dane

Breed	First brought to Britain	Purpose or origin
		bear-hunting in Scandinavia
English Foxhound	13th century	Fox-hunting
English Setter	16th century	Working dog
English Springer Spaniel	Ancient breed	Flushing and retrieving
Fox Terrier (Smooth-haired)	1870s	Working dog
Fox Terrier (Wire-haired)	Very old breed	Fox-bolting
French Bulldog	1902	Sporting dog
Golden Retriever	1870s	Working dog
Great Dane	18th century	Fighting dog, once used for boar-hunting
Greyhound	Ancient breed	Racing and coursing

Breed	First brought to Britain	Purpose or origin
Griffon	1880	Toy dog from Brussels
Harrier	1745	Hare-hunting
Husky	—	Sled-dog
Irish Setter	Indigenous to Ireland	Working dog
Irish Wolfhound	Indigenous to Ireland	Wolf-hunting
Keeshond	Early 20th century	Dutch barge dog
Kelpie	—	Australian sheep dog
Kerry Blue Terrier	Indigenous to Ireland	Sheep-herding
King Charles Spaniel	Before 17th century	Decoration
Labrador Retriever	Early 19th century	Retrieving and as guide dogs
Manchester Terrier	Indigenous	Sporting dog
Mastiff	Introduced by Romans	Fighting, bear-baiting

Pekingese

152

Breed	First brought to Britain	Purpose or origin
Norfolk Terrier	1870-1880	Sporting dog
Norwich Terrier	Descended from Irish terriers	Fox and badger working
Old English Sheepdog	Ancient breed	Sheep-herding
Otterhound	13th century	Otter-hunting
Pekingese	1860	Toy dog
Pointer	19th century	Pointing to birds
Pomeranian	1880s	Toy dog of Arctic origin
Poodle	18th century	Water dog
Poodle (Miniature)	20th century	Decoration
Pug	1688	Toy dog
Pyrenean Mountain dog	1910	Protecting sheep
Rhodesian Ridgeback	—	Lion-hunting
St. Bernard	19th century	Rescuing people lost in Alps
Saluki	1850s	Gazelle-hunting
Samoyed	1889	Rounding-up reindeer, sled dog
Scottish Terrier	Indigenous to Scotland	Sporting dog
Sealyham Terrier	Created 1851	Badger-baiting
Shetland Sheepdog	Indigenous to Shetlands	Sheep and pony herding
Sky Terrier	Old Scottish breed	Fox-holing
Staffordshire Bull Terrier	Indigenous	Sporting dog
Sussex Spaniel	First bred 18th century	Gundog
Welsh Corgi	Indigenous to Wales	Cattle-herding
Welsh Sheepdog	Indigenous to North Wales	Sheep-herding
Welsh Springer Spaniel	10th century	Working dog, both in water and on land
Whippet	1894	Racing
Yorkshire Terrier	Developed 1860s	Rat-catcher

Breeds of Cats

Breed

Long-haired	*Characteristics*
Black	Large round orange eyes, broad head, tufted ears, jet-black coat.
White (blue-eyed)	Pure white colouring, round, broad head, deep blue eyes.
White (orange-eyed)	Similar to above, but with orange eyes.
Blue Persian	Any shade of blue, thick, soft fur, deep orange eyes, short full tail.
Red Self	Deep rich red without markings, copper eyes, long silky coat. Rare in Britain.
Cream	Pale to medium cream colour without markings, silky coat, copper eyes.
Smoke	Black coat shading to silver, white undercoat, orange or copper eyes, bushy tail.
Silver Tabby	Silver with jet-black markings, green or hazel eyes, short bushy tail.
Brown Tabby	Tawny sable colouring with delicate black markings, large round hazel or copper eyes, short full tail.

Brown Tabby

Long-haired	Characteristics
Red Tabby	Deep, rich red colour, bold markings, short, flowing tail with no white tip, deep copper eyes.
Chinchilla	Pure white undercoat, coat on back, flanks, head, ears and tail tipped with black, emerald or blue-green eyes, short bushy tail.
Tortoise-shell	Well-patched coat of black, red and cream, deep orange or copper eyes.
Tortoise-shell-and-white	Black, red and cream well distributed and interspersed with white, deep orange or copper eyes.
Blue-Cream	Intermingled pastel shades of blue and cream, dense coat, deep copper or orange eyes.
Any other	Any cat which does not conform to the standards laid down for a particular breed.
Colourpoint	Long cream hair, dark points and masks, round blue eyes—Siamese-type colouring but it is not a long-haired Siamese.

Short-haired	Characteristics
White	Pure white coat, deep sapphire blue eyes.
Black	Jet-black with no white hairs, orange eyes.
British Blue	Even-coloured light to medium blue coat, copper, orange or yellow eyes.
Russian Blue	Medium to dark blue coat, long, lithe body, narrow head, vivid green eyes.
Cream	Rich cream coat with no white, copper or hazel eyes.
Silver Tabby	Dense black markings on silver ground, eyes green or hazel.
Red Tabby	Rich red coat with dense, dark red markings, hazel or orange eyes.
Brown Tabby	Rich sable or brown coat with black markings, orange, hazel, deep yellow or green eyes.
Tortoise-shell	Equally balanced red and black coat, no white, eyes orange, copper or hazel.
Tortoise-shell-and-white	Clearly-defined dark and light red and black coat equally balanced with white, orange, copper or hazel eyes.
Abyssinian	Ruddy brown coat with two or three bands of black or brown, long pointed head, green, yellow or hazel eyes.

Short-haired	Characteristics
Siamese, seal-pointed	Cream coat, shading to fawn on the back, seal brown points, long tapering tail, slanting brilliant blue eyes.
Siamese blue-pointed	Glacial white coat, shading to blue on back, blue points, eyes bright, vivid blue.
Siamese, chocolate-pointed	Ivory coat, milk chocolate points, clear, vivid blue eyes.
Siamese, lilac-pointed	Frosty-white body, pinkish-grey points, vivid blue eyes.
Manx	Rounded rump with no tail, not even a stump, short back, soft thick coat.
Any other variety	Any cat which does not conform to the standards laid down for a particular breed.
Burmese	Dark seal brown body, shading to lighter colour on chest and stomach. No white or tabby markings. Yellow slanting eyes.
Blue Burmese	Bluish-grey body, yellowish green eyes.
Blue-Cream	Intermingled blue and cream coat with no patches, copper, orange or yellow eyes.
Chestnut Brown Foreign	Even-coloured rich chestnut brown coat, long lithe body, slanting green eyes.

Manx

Jewels

Stone	Main colour	Where found	Outstanding examples
Diamond	Blue-white	Australia, Brazil, Congo, India, Indonesia, Liberia, Sierra Leone, U.S.A., South, South-West and East Africa	Cullinan, found at Pretoria, S. Africa, 1905. 3,106 carats. Cullinan I or Star of Africa, cut from above, now in British Royal Sceptre. 530.2 carats Koh-i-noor, British Crown Jewels, 106 carats cut Hope Diamond, found in India before 1642, now in Smithsonian Institute, Washington D.C., America
Ruby	Dark red	Brazil, Burma, Ceylon, Siam	Largest found: 1,184-carat stone from Burma
Sapphire	Dark blue	Australia, Burma, Ceylon, Kashmir, U.S.A.	Star of India, found in Ceylon, now in the American Museum of Natural History, New York. 563.5 carats
Alexandrite	Dull green in daylight, blood red in artificial light	Brazil, Moravia, U.S.A., U.S.S.R.	
Topaz	Brownish	Australia, Brazil, Ceylon, Germany, S.W. Africa, U.S.S.R.	Largest found: 270 kg. from Brazil
Emerald	Vivid green	Austria, Colombia, Norway, U.S.A., U.S.S.R.	Largest found: 1,350 carats from Colombia
Aquamarine	Pale blue	Austria, Brazil, Colombia, Norway, U.S.A., U.S.S.R.	Largest found: 61 kg. from Brazil

Stone	Main colour	Where found	Outstanding examples
Garnet	Deep purple-red, green, black	India, Ceylon, U.S.A., U.S.S.R.	
Zircon	Usually colourless, can be blue or red-brown	Australia, Burma, Ceylon, India, North America, Siam, U.S.S.R.	
Rock Crystal	Colourless	Brazil, Burma, France, Madagascar, Switzerland, U.S.A.	Largest found: 48 kg. from Burma, now in the U.S. National Museum, Washington
Rose Quartz	Pale pink	Bavaria, Brazil, Finland, S.W. Africa, U.S.A., U.S.S.R.	
Cairngorm	Smoky yellow to brown	Brazil, Madagascar, Manchuria, Scotland, Switzerland, U.S.A., U.S.S.R.	
Amethyst	Purple	Brazil, Ceylon, Germany, Madagascar, Uruguay, U.S.S.R.	
Jade	Green	Burma, China, Tibet	
Cornelian	Blood-red to yellowish-brown	Widespread including Great Britain	
Agate	White to pale grey, blue	Brazil, Germany, India, Madagascar, Scotland	
Onyx	Black and white banded agate	South America, India, U.S.A.	
Jasper	Brown, red, yellow	Egypt, India	
Peridot	Green	Australia, Brazil, Burma, Norway, Red Sea	
Bloodstone	Dark green with red spots	Egypt, India	
Moonstone	Iridescent white to blue	Brazil, Burma, Ceylon	

Stone	Main colour	Where found	Outstanding examples
Opal	Rainbow colours on white ground	Australia, Mexico	Largest found: Olympic Australis, 4.054 kg., Australia
Turquoise	Sky blue	Egypt, Iran, Turkey, U.S.A.	
Lapis Lazuli	Deep azure blue	Afghanistan, Chile, Tibet, U.S.S.R.	
Amber	Clear and cloudy yellow	Baltic and Sicilian coasts	
Coral	Mainly red	Australasia, Pacific and Indian Oceans	
Pearl	Milky white	Western Pacific	Largest found: Hope Pearl, 85 g., 11.4 cm. circumference

The Zodiac

The Zodiac is an imaginary belt in the heavens in which the paths of the sun, moon and major planets are supposed to lie. This is divided into 12 equal parts, each with its own Sign. Astrologers believe that the position of the sun, moon and planets within these Signs at the time of a person's birth has an effect on that person's character and destiny.

The Signs are:

Aries	The Ram	March 21 to April 19
Taurus	The Bull	April 20 to May 20
Gemini	The Twins	May 21 to June 21
Cancer	The Crab	June 22 to July 22
Leo	The Lion	July 23 to August 22
Virgo	The Virgin	August 23 to September 22
Libra	The Scales	September 23 to October 23

Signs of the Zodiac

Aries

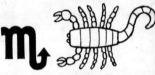

Libra

Taurus

Scorpio

Gemini

Sagittarius

Cancer

Capricorn

Leo

Aquarius

Virgo

Pisces

160

Scorpio	The Scorpion	October 24 to November 21
Sagittarius	The Archer	November 22 to December 21
Capricorn	The Goat	December 22 to January 19
Aquarius	The Water-carrier	January 20 to February 18
Pisces	The Fish	February 19 to March 20

The Meaning of Christian Names

Abraham (boy)	Hebrew	"Father of a multitude"
Abigail (girl)	Hebrew	"Father's joy"
Ada (girl)	Teutonic	Probably means "Happy"
Adam (boy)	Hebrew	"Man"
Adela, Adelaide, Adeline (girl)	Teutonic	"Noble"
Adrian (boy)	Latin	"Black, of the Adriatic"
Agatha (girl)	Greek	"Good"
Agnes (girl)	Greek	"Pure"
Allen, Allan, Alan (boy)	Celtic	"Harmony"
Alastair (boy)	Scottish	Version of Greek Alexander
Albert (boy)	Old German	"Glorious"
Alberta (girl)		Feminine of above
Alexander (boy)	Greek	"Defender of men"
Alexandra (girl)		Feminine of above
Alexis (boy)	Greek	"Helper, defender"
Alfred (boy)	Old English	"Wise counsel"
Algernon (boy)	Old French	"Bewhiskered"
Alice (girl)	Old German	"Truth"
Alwyn, Aylwyn (boy)	Teutonic	"Noble friend"

161

GHB–F

Name	Origin	Meaning
Amabel (girl)	Latin	"Lovable"
Amanda (girl)	Latin	"Worthy of love"
Ambrose (boy)	Greek	"Immortal"
Amelia (girl)	Teutonic	"Energetic"
Amos (boy)	Hebrew	"Strong and courageous"
Anastasia (girl)	Greek	"Resurrection"
Andrea (girl)	Italian	Feminine of Andrew
Andrew (boy)	Greek	"Manly"
Angela (girl)	Greek	"Angelic"
Angus (boy)	Scottish	"Most virtuous"
Ann, Anna,		
Anne (girl)	Hebrew	"Grace"
Annabel (girl)	Celtic	"Grace"
Anthea (girl)	Greek	"Lady of flowers"
Anthony (boy)	Latin	"Inestimable"
Antoinette,		
Antonia (girl)		Feminine of above
Arabella (girl)	Scottish	"Yielding to prayer"
Archibald		
(boy)	Teutonic	"Bold"
Arnold (boy)	Teutonic	"Strong as an eagle"
Arthur (boy)	Celtic	"Of noble race"
Aubrey (boy)	Old German	"Fairy-king"
Audrey (girl)	Anglo-Saxon	"Nobly famous"
Augustus (boy)	Latin	"Majestic"
Augusta (girl)		Feminine of above
Avis (girl)	Latin	"Bird"
Barbara (girl)	Latin	"Strange"
Barnaby (boy)	Hebrew	"Son of exhortation"
Barry (boy)	Celtic	"Looking straight"
Bartholomew		
(boy)	Hebrew	"Warlike"
Basil (boy)	Greek	"King"
Beatrice (girl)	Latin	"Giver of you, blessed"
Belinda (girl)	Old German	"Serpent"
Benedict (boy)	Latin	"Blessed"
Benjamin (boy)	Hebrew	"Son of the right hand"
Bernice (girl)	Greek	"Bringer of victory"
Bernard (boy)	German	"Brave as a bear"
Bertha (girl)	Teutonic	"Bright one"
Bertram (boy)	Teutonic	"Bright raven"
Beryl (girl)	Greek	"Precious stone"
Blanche (girl)	French	"White"
Boris (boy)	Russian	"Warrior"
Brenda (girl)	Scandinavian	"Flame"
Brian (boy)	Celtic	"Strong"
Bridget (girl)	Celtic	"Shining bright"
Bronwen (girl)	Celtic	"White-breasted"

Bruce (boy)	Old French	"Meaning unknown"
Caleb (boy)	Hebrew	"Bold"
Camilla (girl)	Latin	"Sacrificial attendant"
Carol, Caroline (girl)	French	"Noble spirit"
Cassandra (girl)	Greek	"Helper of men"
Catherine (girl)	Latin	"Pure"
Cecil (boy)	Greek	"Blind"
Cecilia, Cecily (girl)		Feminine of Cecil
Cedric (boy)	Teutonic	"Chieftain"
Celia (girl)	Latin	"Heavenly"
Charles (boy)	Teutonic	"Noble spirit"
Charlotte (girl)		Feminine of above
Charmian (girl)	Greek	"Joyful"
Chloe (girl)	Greek	"Green, summery"
Christine (girl)	Old English	"Follower of Christ"
Christopher (boy)	Greek	"Bearer of Christ"
Clara, Clare (girl)	Latin	"Illustrious"
Clarence (boy)	Latin	"Renowned"
Claud, Claude (boy)	Latin	"Lame"
Claudia (girl)		Feminine of above
Clifford (boy)	Teutonic	"Dweller on a slope"
Clive (boy)		Contraction of above
Colin (boy)	Latin	"Dove"
Conrad (boy)	Teutonic	"Able counsel"
Constance (girl)	Latin	"Firm, constant"
Cora (girl)	Greek	"Maiden"
Cornelia (girl)	Latin	"Regal"
Crispin (boy)	Latin	"Curly-haired"
Cuthbert (boy)	Teutonic	"Famous splendour"
Cynthia (girl)	Greek	"Belonging to Mount Cynthus"
Cyril (boy)	Greek	"Lordly"
Dagmar (girl)	Danish	"Dane's joy"
Daisy (girl)	Anglo-Saxon	"Eye of day"
Daniel (boy)	Hebrew	"Divine judge"
Daphne (girl)	Greek	"Bay-tree"
David (boy)	Hebrew	"Beloved"
Dawn (girl)	Modern name	"Daybreak"
Deborah (girl)	Hebrew	"Eloquent"
Deirdre (girl)	Celtic	"Raging one"

Delia (girl)	Greek	Surname of goddess Diana
Denis (boy)	Greek	"Belonging to god of wine, Dionysus"
Denise (girl)	Teutonic	Feminine of above
Derek (boy)	Celtic	"Gift of God"
Desmond (boy)	Latin	Originally a clan-name
Diana (girl)	Latin	Name of Roman goddess of moon, forest and animals
Dinah (girl)	Hebrew	"Judged"
Dolores (girl)	Spanish	"Grief"
Dominic (boy)	Latin	"Born on the Lord's day"
Donald (boy)	Gaelic	"Ruler of the world"
Dora (girl)		Contraction of Dorothea
Dorcas (girl)	Greek	"Gazelle"
Doreen (girl)	Celtic	"Sullen"
Doris (girl)	Greek	Meaning unknown
Dorothea, Dorothy (girl)	Greek	"Gift of God"
Douglas (boy)	Celtic	"Dark stream"
Drusilla (girl)	Latin	Feminine version of "strong man"
Dudley (boy)	English	Taken from a town in Worcestershire
Duncan (boy)	Celtic	"Brown warrior"
Dylan (boy)	Welsh	"The sea"
Ebenezer (boy)	Hebrew	"Stone of help"
Edgar (boy)	Anglo-Saxon	"Fortunate spear"
Edith (girl)	Anglo-Saxon	"Rich gift"
Edmund (boy)	Anglo-Saxon	"Happy protector"
Edna (girl)	Hebrew	"Rich guardian"
Edward (boy)	Anglo-Saxon	"Rich friend"
Edwin (boy)	Anglo-Saxon	"Pleasure"
Egbert (boy)	Anglo-Saxon	"Formidably bright"
Eileen (girl)	Irish form of Helen	
Elaine (girl)	French form of Helen	
Eleanor (girl)	Form of Helen	
Elizabeth (girl)	Hebrew	"Consecrated to God"
Ellen (girl)	Scottish form of Helen	
Elsie (girl)	Contraction of Elizabeth	
Elvira (girl)	Old German	"Elf-counsel"
Emily (girl)	Old French	"Industrious"
Emma (girl)	Teutonic	"Maid of the nation"
Enid (girl)	Celtic	"Spotless, pure"
Enoch (boy)	Hebrew	"Dedicated"
Eric (boy)	Norse	"Ever king"
Erica (girl)	Feminine of above	
Ernest (boy)	Teutonic	"Grave, serious"

Esau (boy)	Hebrew	"Hairy"
Esmê (girl)	French	"Esteemed"
Esther (girl)	Persian	"Star"
Ethel (girl)	Greek	"Noble"
Eugene (boy)	Anglo-Saxon	"Well-born"
Eugenie (girl)	Feminine of Eugene	
Eunice (girl)	Greek	"Happy victory"
Eustace (boy)	Greek	"Happy harvest"
Eva, Eve (girl)	Hebrew	"Life"
Evan (boy)	Celtic	"Young warrior"
Evelyn (boy and girl)	Celtic	"Pleasant"
Ezra (boy)	Hebrew	"Help"
Faith (girl)	English	Self-explanatory
Felicity (girl)	Latin	"Happiness"
Felix (boy)	Latin	"Happy"
Ferdinand (boy)	Teutonic	"Adventurous"
Fergus (boy)	Celtic	"Man's strength"
Fenella (girl)	Celtic	"White-shouldered"
Fingal (boy)	Celtic	"Fair stranger"
Fiona (girl)	Celtic	"White girl"
Flavia (girl)	Latin	"Golden"
Flora (girl)	Latin	"Flower"
Florence (girl)	Latin	"Blooming"
Frances (girl)	Old German	"Free"
Francis (boy)	Masculine of above	
Frederick (boy)	Old German	"Peaceful ruler"
Gabriel (boy)	Hebrew	"Man of God"
Gabrielle (girl)	Feminine of above	
Gareth (boy)	Anglo-Saxon	"Firm spear"
Geoffrey (boy)	Teutonic	"God's peace"
George (boy)	Greek	"Farmer"
Georgina (girl)	Feminine of above	
Gerald (boy)	Teutonic	"Strong in battle"
Geraldine (girl)	Feminine of above	
Gertrude (girl)	Teutonic	"Spear maiden"
Gervase (boy)	Teutonic	"Spear-bearer"
Gideon (boy)	Hebrew	"Mighty warrior"
Gilbert (boy)	Old German	"Bright pledge"
Giles (boy)	Greek	Meaning unknown
Gillian (girl)	Feminine of Julian	
Gladys (girl)	Celtic	"Lame"
Gloria (girl)	Latin	"Fame"
Godfrey (boy)	Teutonic	"God's peace"
Gordon (boy)	Scottish	"From the three-cornered hill"

Grace (girl)	Latin	"Thanks"
Graham (boy)	Greek	"From the grey house"
Gregory (boy)	Celtic	"Watchman"
Guy (boy)	Old German	"Leader"
Gwendoline (girl)	Celtic	"White-browed"
Gwynneth (girl)	Welsh	"Blessed"
Hamish (boy)	Scottish form of James	
Hannah (girl)	Hebrew	"Grace"
Harold (boy)	Norse	"Great general"
Harriet (girl)	Teutonic	"Home-rule"
Harvey (boy)	Celtic	"Bitter"
Hazel (girl)	English	From the tree
Heather (girl)	English	From the plant
Hector (boy)	Greek	"Defender"
Helen (girl)	Greek	"Light"
Henry (boy)	Old German	"Home-rule"
Henrietta (girl)	Old German	Feminine of above
Herbert (boy)	Teutonic	"Bright army"
Hercules (boy)	Greek	"Lordly fame"
Hero (girl)	Greek	"Mistress of the house"
Hilary (boy and girl)	Latin	"Cheerful"
Hilda (girl)	Teutonic	"Battle-maid"
Honor (girl)	Latin	"Honour"
Hope (girl)	English	Self-explanatory
Horace (boy)	Latin	"Punctual"
Howard (boy)	Old French	"Guardian of the sword"
Hubert (boy)	Teutonic	"Bright of mind"
Hugh (boy)	Teutonic	"Spirit"
Humphrey (boy)	Teutonic	"Great peace"
Hyacinth (girl)	Greek	"Purple"
Ian (boy)	Scottish form of John	
Ida (girl)	Teutonic	"Labour"
Imogen (girl)	Anglo-Saxon	"Daughter"
Ira (girl)	Hebrew	"Messenger of peace"
Irene (girl)	Greek	"Watchful"
Iris (girl)	Greek	"Rainbow"
Isaac (boy)	Hebrew	"Laughter"
Isabel, Isobel (girl)	Same as Elizabeth	
Ivan (boy)	Russian form of John	
Ivor (boy)	Norse	"Protector of Ing"
Ivy (girl)	Teutonic	"Clinging"

Jacob (boy)	Hebrew	"Supplanter"
Jacqueline (girl)	French	Feminine of James
James (boy)	Hebrew	"Supplanter"
Jane (girl)	Feminine of John	
Janet (girl)	Same as Jane	
Janice (girl)	Hebrew	"Gift of God"
Jean (girl)	Same as above	
Jemima (girl)	Hebrew	"Dove"
Jennifer (girl)	Celtic	"White vision"
Jeremy (boy)	Hebrew	"Appointed by God"
Jessica (girl)	Hebrew	"The Lord watches"
Jill (girl)	Contraction of Gillian	
Joan (girl)	Hebrew	"Grace of God"
Joanna (girl)	Hebrew	"Grace of God"
Jocelyn (boy and girl)	Teutonic	Meaning unknown
Joel (boy)	Hebrew	"The Lord is God"
John (boy)	Hebrew	"Grace of God"
Jonathan (boy)	Hebrew	"God's gift"
Joseph (boy)	Hebrew	"He shall increase"
Josephine (girl)	Feminine of above	
Joshua (boy)	Hebrew	"Lord of salvation"
Joyce (girl)	Celtic	From the name of Breton St. Josse
Jude, Judas (boy)	Hebrew	"Praise of the Lord"
Judith (girl)	Hebrew	"Praised"
Julia (girl)	Latin	Feminine of Julius
Juliet (girl)	Contraction of Julia	
Julian (boy)	Same as Julius	
Julius (boy)	Greek	"Soft-haired"
June (girl)	English	Taken from the month
Justin (boy)	Latin	"Just"
Karen (girl)	Danish	"Pure"
Katherine, Kathleen (girl)	Greek	"Pure"
Keith (boy)	Gaelic	"Wind"
Kenneth (boy)	Celtic	"Handsome"
Kevin (boy)	Irish version of Kenneth	
Lana (girl)	Greek	"Light"
Lancelot (boy)	Latin	"Boy-servant"
Laura (girl)	Latin	"Laurel tree"
Laurence, Lawrence (boy)	Greek	"Laurel tree"

167

Lavinia (girl)	Latin	"Woman from Lavinium"
Leander (boy)	Greek	"Lion-man"
Leigh, Lee (boy)	Anglo-Saxon	"Meadow"
Leila (girl)	Arabic	"Darkness"
Leo (boy)	Latin	"Lion"
Leonard (boy)	Teutonic	"Brave as a lion"
Leopold (boy)	Old German	"Bold people"
Lesley (girl)	Feminine of Leslie	
Leslie (boy)	English	Meaning unknown
Letitia (girl)	Latin	"Gladness"
Lewis (boy)	Celtic	"Lion-like"
Lilian (girl)	English	Meaning unknown
Linda (girl)	Old German	"Snake-like"
Lionel (boy)	Greek	"Little lion"
Llewellyn (boy)	Welsh	"Lion-like"
Lloyd (boy)	Celtic	"Grey"
Lorna (girl)	Anglo-Saxon	"Love-lorn"
Louise (girl)	French feminine form of Lewis	
Louis (boy)	French masculine form of Lewis	
Lucy (girl)	Latin	"Born in daylight"
Luke (boy)	Greek	"Light"
Lydia (girl)	Greek	"A woman of Lydia"
Lynn (girl)	Anglo-Saxon	"Cascade"
Mabel (girl)	Latin	"Lovable"
Madeleine (girl)	Hebrew	"Woman of Magdala"
Madoc (boy)	Welsh	"Fortunate"
Madge (girl)	Short for Margaret	
Magnus (boy)	Latin	"Great"
Maisie (girl)	Short for Margaret	
Malcolm (boy)	Celtic	"Servant of Columba"
Manfred (boy)	Old German	"Man of peace"
Marcus (boy)	Latin	"God of war"
Margaret (girl)	English	"A pearl"
Maria (girl)	English	Early form of Mary
Marion (girl)	Greek	Early form of Mary
Marina (girl)	Latin	"Of the sea"
Marjorie (girl)	Scottish form of Margaret	
Mark (boy)	Same as Marcus	
Marmaduke (boy)	Celtic	"Sea leader"
Martha (girl)	Aramaic	"A lady"
Martin (boy)	Latin	"Belonging to Mars"
Mary (girl)	Hebrew	"Bitterness"
Matilda (girl)	Teutonic	"Mighty battle-maid"

Matthew (boy)	Hebrew	"Gift of the Lord"
Maud (girl)	Same as Matilda	
Maureen (girl)	Irish form of Mary	
Maurice (boy)	Latin	"Dark-skinned"
Mavis (girl)	Old English	"Song-thrush"
Maximilian (boy)	Latin	"Greatest"
May (girl)	Form of Mary	
Melanie (girl)	Greek	"Dark-complexioned"
Meredith (boy)	Welsh	"Sea-protector"
Mervyn (boy)	Anglo-Saxon	"Famous friehd"
Michael (boy)	Hebrew	"Like the Lord"
Mildred (girl)	Teutonic	"Mild power"
Millicent (girl)	Teutonic	"Strong worker"
Minnie (girl)	Teutonic	"Love"
Miranda (girl)	Latin	"Worthy of admiration"
Miriam (girl)	Hebrew	"Rebellion"
Moira (girl)	Celtic	"Soft"
Mona (girl)	Greek	"Unique"
Monica (girl)	Greek	"Unique"
Morgan (boy)	Welsh	"Sea-dweller"
Mortimer (boy)	Celtic	"Sea warrior"
Mungo (boy)	Celtic	"Lovable"
Muriel (girl)	Celtic	"Sea-withe"
Myfanwy (girl)	Celtic	"Child of the water"
Myra (girl)	Contraction of Miranda	
Nancy (girl)	Variation of Ann	
Naomi (girl)	Hebrew	"My fine one"
Natalie (girl)	Latin	"Birth"
Nathaniel (boy)	Hebrew	"Gift of God"
Neil (boy)	Celtic	"Champion"
Neville (boy)	French	"New city"
Nicholas (boy)	Greek	"Victory of the people"
Nigel (boy)	Latin	"Black"
Ninian (boy)	Scottish	Meaning unknown
Noah (boy)	Hebrew	"Rest"
Noel (boy)	French	"Christmas"
Norah (girl)	Irish	"Honour"
Norma (girl)	Latin	"Square"
Norman (boy)	Teutonic	"Norseman"
Obadiah (boy)	Hebrew	"Servant of the Lord"
Octavia (girl)	Latin	"Eighth child"
Odile (girl)	Teutonic	"Of the fatherland"
Olga (girl)	Slavonic	"Holy"

Olive, Olivia (girl)		"An olive tree"
Oliver (boy)	Masculine form of above	
Ophelia (girl)	Greek	"Wisdom"
Osbert (boy)	Teutonic	"Divinely bright"
Oscar (boy)	Old English	"Divine spear"
Oswald (boy)	Anglo-Saxon	"Free of hand"
Owen (boy)	Welsh	"Well-born"
Pamela (girl)	Greek	"Sweetness"
Pascal (boy)	Greek	"Suffering"
Pascoe (boy)	Cornish version of above	
Patricia (girl)	Latin	"Patrician"
Patrick (boy)	Masculine form of above	
Paul (boy)	Latin	"Small"
Pauline (girl)	Feminine form of above	
Penelope (girl)	Greek	"Weaver"
Percival (boy)	French	"Pierce the vale"
Peregrine (boy)	Latin	"Wanderer"
Perdita (girl)	Latin	"Lost"
Peter (boy)	Greek	"Stone"
Petronella (girl)	Feminine form of Peter	
Philip (boy)	Greek	"Lover of horses"
Philippa (girl)	Feminine form of above	
Phoebe (girl)	Greek	"Radiant"
Phyllis (girl)	Greek	"Green leaf or bough"
Piers (boy)	Old English form of Peter	
Polly (girl)	Short for Mary	
Priscilla (girl)	Latin	"Of olden times"
Prudence (girl)	Latin	"Prudent"
Prunella (girl)	Old French	"Plum-coloured"
Quentin (boy)	Latin	"Fifth child"
Rachel (girl)	Hebrew	"A ewe"
Ralph (boy)	Old English	"Wolf"
Randolph (boy)	Old English	"House-wolf"
Raoul (boy)	French form of above	
Raphael (boy)	Hebrew	"Healed by God"
Raymond (boy)	Old French	"Wise protection"
Rebecca (girl)	Hebrew	"A snare"
Regina (girl)	Latin	"Queen"
Reginald (boy)	Teutonic	"Judgement"
René (boy)	French	"Born again"
Reuben (boy)	Hebrew	"Behold, a son"

Rex (boy)	Latin	"King"
Rhoda (girl)	Greek	"Rose"
Richard (boy)	Old English	"Stern ruler"
Robert (boy)	Old German	"Bright fame"
Roberta (girl)	Feminine form of above	
Robin (boy)	Short for Robert	
Rodney (boy)	Old English	"Famous ruler"
Roderick (boy)	Old German	Meaning unknown
Roger (boy)	Teutonic	"Spear of fame"
Roland (boy)	Teutonic	"Fame of the land"
Roma (girl)	Latin	"Of Rome"
Ronald (boy)	Scottish form of Reginald	
Rory (boy)	Celtic	"Red, ruddy"
Rosalind (girl)	Spanish	"Fair as a rose"
Rosamund (girl)	Teutonic	"Horse-protection"
Rose (girl)	English	"Rose"
Rosemary (girl)	Latin	"Mist of the sea"
Rowena (girl)	Celtic	"White skirt"
Roy (boy)	Celtic	"Red"
Rudolph (boy)	Teutonic	"Wolf-fame"
Rufus (boy)	Latin	"Red-haired"
Rupert (boy)	Teutonic	"Bright fame"
Ruth (girl)	Hebrew	"Vision of beauty"
Sadie (girl)	Short for Sarah	
Sally (girl)	Short for Sarah	
Samuel (boy)	Hebrew	"Name of God"
Sarah (girl)	Hebrew	"Princess"
Sean (boy)	Irish form of John	
Sebastian (boy)	Greek	"Venerated"
Selwyn (boy)	Old English	"House friend"
Serena (girl)	Latin	"Calm, serene"
Seth (boy)	Hebrew	"Compensation"
Sheila (girl)	Irish form of Celia	
Shirley (girl)	English	Originally, a surname
Sibyl (girl)	Greek	"A prophetess"
Sidney (boy)	English	Contraction of St. Denis
Simon (boy)	Greek	"Snub-nose"
Sonia (girl)	Slavonic	"Wise"
Sophia, Sophie (girl)	Greek	"Wisdom"
Stanley (boy)	English	Derived from a surname
Stella (girl)	Latin	"Star"
Stephanie (girl)	Feminine form of Stephen	
Stephen, Steven (boy)	Greek	"Crown"
Stewart (boy)	Anglo-Saxon	"Steward"
Susan, Susannah (girl)	Hebrew	"Graceful white lily"
Sylvia (girl)	Latin	"Wood-dweller"

Tabitha (girl)	Aramaic	
Tamsin (girl)	Contraction of Thomasina	
Tancred (boy)	Old German	"Grateful speech"
Terence (boy)	Latin	"Tender"
Teresa (girl)	Greek	"Reaper"
Thea (girl)	Greek	"Divine"
Theobald (boy)	Teutonic	"Folk-bold"
Theodore (boy)	Greek	"Gift of God"
Thomas (boy)	Aramaic	"Twin"
Timothy (boy)	Greek	"Honouring God"
Tobias, Toby (boy)	Hebrew	"God is good"
Tristram (boy)	Celtic	"A herald"
Ulric (boy)	Old English	"Wolf-rule"
Ulysses (boy)	Greek	"Hater"
Una, Oonagh (girl)	Latin	"The one"
Urian (boy)	Hebrew	"The Lord is my light"
Ursula (girl)	Latin	"She-bear"
Valentine (boy and girl)	Latin	"Strong"
Valerie (girl)	Latin	"Strong, healthy"
Vanessa (girl)	English	Meaning unknown
Vera (girl)	Latin	"True"
Vernon (boy)	Latin	"Flourishing"
Veronica (girl)	Latin	"Way of truth"
Victor (boy)	Latin	"Victorious"
Victoria (girl)	Feminine form of above	
Vincent (boy)	Latin	"Conquering"
Virgil (boy)	Latin	"Flourishing"
Virginia (girl)	Latin	"Of the spring"
Vivian (boy)	Latin	"Alive"
Wallace (boy)	Derived form of Scottish surname	
Walter (boy)	Old German	"Folk-ruler"
Wanda (girl)	Old German	"Stem, stock"
Watten (boy)	Teutonic	"Protecting friend"
Wendy (girl)	Teutonic	"Wanderer"
Wilfred (boy)	Anglo-Saxon	"Resolute peace"
William (boy)	Teutonic	"Helmet of resolution"
Winifred (girl)	Celtic	"White wave"
Winston (boy)	English	Originally a place-name
Xavier (boy)	Arabic	"Splendid"
Yolande (girl)	French	"Violet"
Yvonne (girl)	French feminine form of John	

Zachary (boy)	Hebrew	"Remembered by the Lord"
Zallah (girl)	Hebrew	"Shadow"
Zoë (girl)	Greek	"Life"
Zuleika (girl)	Arabic	"Fair"

Nature Study

Wild Animals of Britain
Insectivores (insect-eating mammals)

Name	Habitat
Hedgehog	Open country with some cover, gardens and parks throughout Britain
Mole	Found everywhere, except on barren mountains, in sand and conifer forests
Common Shrew (Ranny)	Widespread, particularly in dense herbage in woods, hedgerows and scrub
Pigmy Shrew	Smallest mammal in Britain. Found everywhere
Water Shrew	Nocturnal. Found in clear streams, especially watercress beds
Lesser White-Toothed Shrew	Only in Isles of Scilly and Channel Islands

Bats

Pipistrelle	Smallest British bat. Rock crevices, trees and buildings
Long-Eared Bat	Congregates in summer in trees and buildings. Hibernates singly in caves and buildings
Noctule	Buildings and trees everywhere
Daubenton's Bat	Lives in large groups in summer in buildings, caves and trees
Leisler's Bat	Hollow trees and buildings

Name	Habitat
Barbastrelle	Woodland areas only
Natterer's Bat	Mainly in woods
Whiskered Bat	Common in England, Wales and Ireland. Rare in Scotland. Buildings and trees in summer, rocks, cellars and caves in winter
Greater Horseshoe Bat	Lofts and attics in summer, caves in winter
Lesser Horseshoe Bat	Habitat similar to Greater Horseshoe Bat
Serotine	Buildings and hollow trees
Bechstein's Bat	Very rare. Hollow trees in summer, caves in winter
Mouse-eared Bat	Only in caves and buildings in Dorset
Rabbits and Hares	
Rabbit	Introduced into Britain by the Normans. Widespread in woods and grassland, though their numbers were greatly reduced by the outbreaks of myxomatosis in the 1950s
Brown Hare	A few in Scotland and Ireland but mainly in open country on chalk and limestone, below 610 metres
Mountain (Blue) Hare	Open moors and rocky slopes of Scottish Highlands and Ireland
Rodents	
Red Squirrel	Conifer forests, particularly the Scots Pine. Growing rarer
American Grey Squirrel	Brought to this country between 1876 and 1929. Woodland, particularly oaks
Harvest Mouse	Inhabited buildings, corn ricks, hedgerows
Wood Mouse	Hedgerows and woods everywhere
Yellow-necked Mouse	Hedgerows and woods everywhere
House Mouse	Britain's smallest mouse. Hedgerows and cornfields
Edible Dormouse	Deciduous wood and lofts of buildings in Buckinghamshire and Oxfordshire. Introduced into Britain in 1902
Dormouse	Woodland, particularly containing beech and hazel trees
Bank Vole	Deciduous woods, scrub and

Name	Habitat
	hedgerows. Sometimes on open ground below 790 metres
Orkney Vole	Pastures and arable land everywhere
Short-Tailed Vole	Rough grassland
Water Vole (Water Rat)	Banks of lowland canals, ponds, slow-running rivers and Highland burns below 610 metres
Coypu (Nutria)	Introduced about 1930. Became wild after escaping from fur farms. River banks, reed beds and marshes in East Anglia
Black Rat	Very common in Britain in Middle Ages and is thought to have brought the Black Death to Europe. Rare since 1700 except around ports where it arrives in ships
Brown Rat	Came to Britain in 18th century. Buildings, refuse tips, corn ricks, sewers

Carnivores (flesh-eating mammals)

Name	Habitat
Pine Marten	Rare. High woods and rock slopes
American Mink	After escaping from fur farms, now breeds in the wild near rivers, streams and lakes in Devon
Polecat	Thickets and woods in Wales
Wild Cat	Woods and moorland in Highlands
Red Fox	Widespread throughout Britain in any kind of country
Stoat	Widespread. Any kind of country
Weasel	Widespread. Any kind of country
Badger	Woods and copses near pasture-land everywhere except Scottish isles, parts of Scotland, north-west England, East Anglia and parts of Wales
Common Otter	Streams, lakes and marshes, particularly along the western coasts of Scotland, England, Wales and Ireland. Very rare in south and south-east England

Seals

Name	Habitat
Grey (Atlantic) Seal	Stormy waters on islands and rocky shores with access to open sea
Common (Harbour) Seal	Sheltered water, mud and sandbanks, estuaries

Name	Habitat
Deer	
Red Deer	Largest native deer. Indigenous to the Lake District, Brendon and Quantock Hills, Scottish Highlands and isles, County Kerry and Exmoor. Moves from forest to moorland in summer
Roe Deer	Open woodland and on the edge of forests. Mainly in Surrey, Sussex, Border Counties, Scotland and the Lake District
Fallow Deer	New Forest, Rockingham Forest and Epping Forests. Deer which have escaped from parks choose deciduous or mixed woods
Japanese Sika Deer	Introduced into parks in mid-18th century. Prefer deciduous or mixed woods with hazel and bracken cover
Indian Muntjac (Barking Deer) and Chinese Muntjac	Woods in and around Bedfordshire
Chinese Water Deer	Escaped from Woburn Park, Bedfordshire, and settled in woodland and grassland nearby
Reindeer	Once native to Britain but became extinct here in 13th century. Recently, reindeer from Swedish Lapland have been introduced into the Cairngorms, Scotland
Wild Goat	Mountain crags and inaccessible rock ledges in Scotland, northern England and Wales
Wild Soay Sheep	Only on the islands of St. Kilda
White Cattle	Chillingham Park, Northumberland. Descended from wild forest cattle which were domesticated in the 13th century
Wild Pony	Strictly speaking, not wild as they are regularly herded and branded. Breeds include Shetland, Welsh, Exmoor, Dartmoor, New Forest, Fell, Highland, Connemara
Snakes	
Grass Snake (Ringed Snake)	Hedgerows, open woodland and marshes. Harmless

Name	Habitat
Smooth Snake	Sandy soils on heath and woodland. Harmless
Adder (Viper)	Dry sandy heaths, open moor and hillsides. Lochs and coves in Highlands. Marshland in East Anglia. Poisonous

Lizards

Viviparous Lizard	Everywhere below 915 metres
Slow-worm (Blind-worm)	Heaths and gardens, particularly in south and west Britain. It is not a snake but a limbless lizard
Sand Lizard	Dry open country, heaths and sand-dunes

Newts

Warty Newt	Deep ponds on clay or chalk
Smooth Newt	Most ponds, except in hills
Palmate Newt	Prefers ponds in hilly country

Toads and Frogs

Common Toad	Beneath stones, in shady places and hollows
Natterjack (Running Toad)	Sandy soil at sea-level
Common (Brown) Frog	Widespread. Usually prefers to be near a pond
Edible Frog	In or near water. Has been found on Ham Common and Hampstead Heath
Marsh Frog	Only in the Rye Marshes and Romney and Walland Marshes

Animal Tracks

The sketches below show some of the most familiar animal tracks. Look for them in dust, soft soil, mud or snow.

Dog

House Cat

Fox

front hind   Bull   Cow

Otter   *Red Deer*

  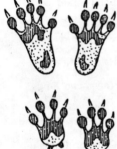

Hedgehog   *Mole*   *Grey Squirrel*

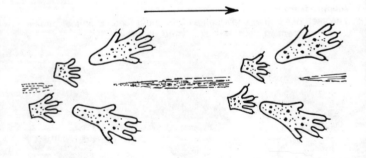

Field Mouse

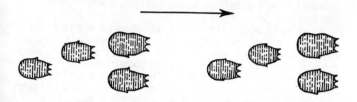

Rabbit

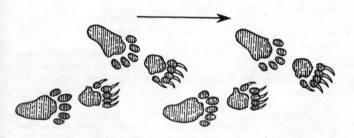

Badger

How to Use the Countryside

Whether you go by bus, train, car or bicycle, a day's outing to the countryside is easily arranged these days. Some of you may already live in the country or on the edge of a town with fields at your back door. Those of you who live in a city may be able to visit the country only occasionally, but wherever you come from the code of the countryside should always be remembered.

1. Where possible, try to stick to established paths and tracks. If you have to cross a field, always avoid going straight across. If you stay close to the fence, you can be sure of not doing any damage to growing crops.
2. Leave all gates as you find them. A closed gate should be closed behind you, an open one left open. When climbing over a gate, do

179

so at the hinge end—it puts less strain on the hinges.

3. Take care not to damage fences and hedges when getting over them.

4. Be careful of livestock. If there is a bull in a field, don't go into the field. No bull can be trusted, particularly with strangers. Never go near a flock of sheep, especially if you have a dog with you. Sheep are easily alarmed and will run away if frightened and it is a great temptation for a frolicsome puppy, however innocent his intentions, to chase after them. In the lambing season (from December to April), a frightened ewe may lose her unborn lamb.

5. If told you are trespassing, apologise and leave at once.

6. Never leave litter. Waste paper, banana skins, old tins, should be collected up, taken home and put in your dustbin. If this is impossible, dig a hole and bury the litter. Quite apart from the unsightly appearance of rubbish scattered round the countryside, sharp tins and broken glass may harm livestock, and abandoned milk or lemonade bottles could start a fire as the rays of the sun, passing through the glass, cause the dry grass beneath to smoulder.

7. Never camp or light a fire on private ground without first asking permission. After camping, clear up properly. Always make certain the fire is out before leaving.

8. Never light a fire on grass or in woodland. Choose a bare patch of earth and, if possible, confine the fire within a circle of stones.

9. Never eat berries unless you know what they are. Some berries are poisonous.

10. It is tempting to pick wild flowers but try not to do so unless you are taking them straight home. To pick a bunch of flowers and throw them away when they have wilted is a senseless way to treat the countryside. Bluebells, incidentally, are best left unpicked. They die very quickly, even if put in water at once.

Care of Your Pets

Cats

Temperament

Most cats are friendly creatures and show pleasure if you talk to them and stroke them, but they are also very independent in character and are often more greatly attached to places than to people. Always handle them gently, stroking them in the direction their fur lies, and avoid picking them up too much and carrying them around. If a cat shows signs of irritability, leave him alone.

Living conditions
A small bed or basket, raised off the floor and with sides to prevent draughts, is best for him to sleep in. Cats like warmth and love stretching out in front of the fire, sleeping in the sun, or sneaking up on to your bed if they get the chance. A cat is happiest if he can go in and out of the house at will, either through a window, which is permanently left open, or through a special hinged flap fitted into the garden door. If you live in a flat or in a busy street, where it would be impossible or dangerous for him to be out on his own, always see that he has a special scratching post, covered with a rough tweedy material, on which he can sharpen his claws.

House-training
Cats are naturally clean and, once house-trained, will be as upset as you if they accidentally make a mess where they know they shouldn't. If he cannot get into the garden, you must provide your cat with a special tray, which should always be kept in the same place, filled with special litter or sawdust and cleaned out regularly. Provided a kitten doesn't leave his mother too young, he will probably be half house-trained by the time he comes to you, for mother cats themselves often teach their kittens how to behave and will be very severe with them if they disobey. A kitten who hasn't learned to use his tray or the garden will generally choose one particular corner of the room, returning to it next time. Discourage him by speaking to him sharply, showing him the proper place and, as a final deterrent, sprinkling pepper on the spot.

Food
Cats can be finicky about their food and often prefer some variety in their diet. Young kittens should have four meals a day, reducing gradually to two or even one by the time they are fully-grown. The amount to give them varies according to the individual cat, but, provided he gets exercise, one tin a day of proprietary cat-food, supplemented with milk, should be sufficient. Vary the diet with raw liver, boiled fish or the pickings from the chicken you had for lunch, but don't give your cat cooked chicken bones and watch out for fish bones. Always see that he has fresh water available, and, if possible, access to fresh grass.

Health
Make certain your cat is inoculated against feline enteritis as soon as he is old enough (about 12 weeks). He will also need worming occasionally and you should ask your vet the best method to choose. If you are at all worried about your cat's health, consult the vet.

On holiday
NEVER leave a cat without making arrangements for someone to come in and feed him regularly. If this is impossible, put him in boarding kennels while you are away.

NEVER leave him with six or seven meals laid out in saucers—even if he doesn't eat himself silly at the first meal, the food will certainly deteriorate later on. If you are only going to be away a short time, during the day, say, so that you will be back in the evening, you may leave him alone in the house quite happily. Cats are normally content to be on their own and only start fretting at mealtimes.

Dogs
Temperament
Dogs are warm, affectionate, faithful animals and, unlike cats, usually prefer people to places. This doesn't mean, of course, that you can treat a dog roughly or push him about without his objecting, but he enjoys being fussed over and responds to discipline and training.

Living conditions
A bed or basket, with his own special rug, in a draught-free spot is a suitable sleeping place for most dogs. An outside kennel is excellent for larger dogs, provided it is out of the wind. The kennel should be airy but not draughty and it is best if it is enclosed in a run, so that the dog is not free to roam the garden at night. Use plenty of straw—not hay—for his bedding and clean the kennel out regularly, burning the old straw.

Training
Puppies take longer to house-train than kittens, but you can save your mother's carpets by taking your puppy out of doors regularly when he is very young. Speak to him severely if he does make a mess in the house and take him into the garden immediately. Don't spank him—the tone of your voice will show that you are displeased. After a few weeks, he will learn to scratch or whine at the door when he wishes to go out. Teach your dog obedience—an untrained dog who is allowed to do as he likes is a nuisance to everyone. Training is not difficult as long as you have patience, and praise him or give him a titbit (a biscuit, not chocolate which is bad for his teeth) when he does well. All dogs should come to a whistle, walk at heel, and sit when told to do so.

Food
Dogs need meat, biscuits or biscuit-meal and a certain amount of green vegetables to keep them healthy. Meat and gravy can be mixed with brown bread if necessary, but do not give your dog white bread. Puppies should be fed four times a day and their diet should include milk. By the time he is a year old, one meal a day is sufficient, and the amount of food varies according to his weight from 70 g. a day for a dog weighing 450 g. to 1.8 kg. a day for a dog weighing 45 kg. Always see that your dog has plenty of fresh water.

Health
Puppies should be inoculated against hard-pad and distemper when they are about three months old, and they will also need worming. Ask your vet about this. Otherwise, keep your dog well-groomed and see that he has enough exercise. Just letting him into the garden is not enough, unless your garden is enormous. He needs a walk every day, preferably in the fields if you live in the country or in a park if you live in town. If he seems to be off-colour or scratches a great deal, see the vet.

On holiday
If you can't take your dog with you, send him to boarding kennels. NEVER leave him in the house alone for a long period, even if you have a friend who can come in to feed him. This doesn't mean that you can't leave him alone for a few hours, especially if he is able to get into the garden, but never leave him alone in the house overnight.

Ponies
Temperament
Provided a pony has been kindly treated in the past, he will be good-tempered, friendly and sociable. A kind nature is essential in a first pony, whatever other faults he may have. He should also be easy to catch, well-mannered in a stable, and completely trustworthy on the road, in traffic and with other ponies.

Living conditions
The native breeds of ponies in Britain are extremely hardy and prefer living out of doors to being kept in a stable, whatever the weather. Their field should be securely fenced and have a constant supply of fresh water. The only shelter they need is a windbreak—a high hedge or the wall of a building—and some kind of protection from the hot sun.

Food
In summer, ponies will live happily on grass and only require extra feeding before and after a particularly hard day. In this case, give them a bran feed, made of bran mixed with water and a little chaff

(chopped hay). Oats—preferably crushed—can be added to the mash but do not give them too much, no more than a double handful. In winter, when the grass has stopped growing, a pony needs hay and a regular feed once or twice a day of boiled barley or dried sugar beet soaked overnight in water, mixed with bran and chaff. Pony nuts are good for them and can be added to the feed. Give your pony oats only if a hard day lies ahead of him. Discourage your pony from drinking straight after a feed. When he comes in hot and tired after a hard ride, offer him a bucket of water *before* you give him his feed.

Health
Care of a pony's feet is vital, and you should take him regularly to a farrier to have his shoes changed. Sometimes, the hoof will have grown too long before the shoe is worn out. In this case, have the shoe removed, the hoof trimmed and the old shoe put back on. Always keep his hooves cleaned out. If a pony cuts himself badly, call the vet at once. Tetanus is a real danger and he will need an injection as soon as possible. Never put your pony in a field or tie him up where he can reach a yew tree or hedge. Yew is deadly poisonous to horses. Ragwort is also dangerous. An old pony, who seems to be having difficulty with his feeding, may need to have his teeth filed. Consult the vet.

Mice
Living conditions
Mice need a cage big enough to give them plenty of room. The smallest size for two or three mice is one 46 cm. long, twenty cm. high and twenty cm. deep. It is better to have a cage 46 cm. high so that it can be fitted with little ladders and swings to keep the mice amused. Never give your mice a revolving wheel. Sprinkle the floor of the cage with sawdust and give the mice a clean bed of hay every week. Once a month, wash out the cage thoroughly with boiling water and a little disinfectant.

Food
In the morning, give each mouse about a tablespoon of oats, coarse oatmeal or canary seed. His evening meal should be a little less corn or seed plus some bread and milk. The bread should be brown or wholemeal, soaked in boiling water, squeezed until nearly dry and mixed with a little fresh milk. A piece of bread the size of a tangerine will be enough for four mice. Always remove any food left by the mice and give them fresh water daily. A little green food, such as dandelion leaves, chickweed, groundsel or lettuce, should be given to them at mid-day.

Rabbits
Living conditions
A rabbit hutch should have two compartments, one for eating and

living in, the other for sleeping. The day compartment should be about 100 cm. wide and the night one about 30 to 46 cm. wide. A partition with an opening in it should separate the two. Cover the front of the day room with a wire netting door and fix an ordinary door to the front of the other room. See that the roof slopes from front to back and projects seven to fifteen cm. over the hutch. The hutch should be raised off the ground and placed out of the midday sun and away from the prevailing wind. The best bedding for rabbits is a layer of peat moss litter, covered with straw or wood chips.

Food
Rabbits like grass, meadow and clover hay and all garden greenstuffs, and need feeding twice a day. Make sure they have plenty of fresh water.

Health
Exercise is necessary for their well-being. A large exercise pen, covered with wire mesh, which can be moved across the lawn, is ideal, but remember to make the pen with a wire mesh base so that the rabbits cannot burrow into the ground and escape. Does make the best pets as they are more friendly than bucks and will live together quite happily.

Golden hamsters
Living conditions
Their cage should be of wood at least 16 mm. thick and measure 61 by 30 by 23 cm. deep. It should have a hinged lid and a glass panel in the front. For cleanliness, a hamster needs sawdust on the floor and a good ball of hay for his bed. He is a very clean creature and does not smell, so his cage can be kept in any room in the house. Never put a hamster in the open, although a warm shed will be all right provided it is mouseproof. Clean his cage out once a week. Always keep hamsters singly, otherwise they may fight.

Food
A hamster needs about a tablespoon of mash a day, given to him in the early evening. Make the mash from small puppy meal mixed with table scraps—bits of meat, boneless fish, bacon rind, cheese, etc. Quaker oats, baked bread, maize or mixed corn may also be given to him, and nuts, raisins or cake are welcome titbits. He also likes the same sort of greenfood given to rabbits. Fresh water is important.

Health
When choosing a hamster, look at his ears. They should be covered with lots of silky hairs, which means he is a young animal, and free from tumours. His body should be plump and well-conditioned and his fur soft and thick. When the weather is cold, a hamster

hibernates like a dormouse and appears quite stiff and dead. Leave him to waken naturally and put some dry food in the cage in case a warm day wakes him up and he feels hungry.

Cage birds
Living conditions
The smallest size of cage necessary is one measuring 91 cm. by 38 cm. by 38 cm. If you have room and can get a larger one, do so, keeping the perches far apart to give the birds as much flying space as possible. Avoid too many knick-knacks which can impede flight, but a few playthings, such as a pingpong ball or cotton reel suspended on a thread, will be appreciated. Birds need company and it is preferable to keep a pair.

Food
Canary seed or a mixture of canary seed and millet makes a good staple diet. Supplement this with a special mixture containing extra protein and vitamins. A cuttlefish bone provides necessary mineral elements. Grit must be given to them, placed in a small pot, and salt in the form of sea sand or as a rock salt put in with the seed. Water must always be available, changed daily.

Health
If you place the cage near a window, make sure that the birds are not in a draught or in the direct rays of the sun. In warm weather, put a saucer of tepid water in the cage so that the birds may splash about in it. If your bird seems off-colour, get expert advice from a vet.

Sport

Olympic Games
Men and men's sports predominate in the Olympic Games. In the 1964 Olympic Games at Tokyo, for example, twenty sports were included but women were allowed to take part in only seven of them—Athletics, Canoeing, Equestrianism, Fencing, Gymnastics, Swimming and Diving and Yachting. The Olympic Games were revived in 1896 and are held every four years at a place fixed by the

International Olympic Committee. Whether the Games are held or not, the numbered sequence remains unaltered. World Wars I and II, for instance, caused the cancellation of the Berlin meeting in 1916, the Tokyo—afterwards allotted to Helsinki—meeting in 1940 and the London meeting in 1944. Here is the full list:

I	1896 Athens	XI	1936 Berlin
II	1900 Paris	XII	1940 Tokyo, Helsinki
III	1904 St. Louis	XIII	1944 London
IV	1908 London	XIV	1948 London
V	1912 Stockholm	XV	1952 Helsinki
VI	1916 Berlin	XVI	1956 Melbourne
VII	1920 Antwerp	XVII	1960 Rome
VIII	1924 Paris	XVIII	1964 Tokyo
IX	1928 Amsterdam	XIX	1968 Mexico City
X	1932 Los Angeles	XX	1972 Munich
		XXI	1976 Montreal

The Winter Olympics were started in 1924 and their venues are as follows:

I	1924 Chamonix	VII	1956 Cortina, Italy
II	1928 St. Moritz	VIII	1960 Squaw Valley, California
III	1932 Lake Placid		
IV	1936 Garmisch-Partenkirchen	IX	1964 Innsbruck
		X	1968 Grenoble
V	1948 St. Moritz	XI	1972 Sapporo, Japan
VI	1952 Oslo	XII	1976 Innsbruck

Countries winning Olympic Medals since 1896:

Name	Gold	Silver	Bronze	Total
1. United States	547	386	345	1,378
2. Great Britain	139	182	155	476
3. Russia (1908 and 1912) (U.S.S.R. since 1952)	181	151	135	467
4. Sweden	123	122	152	397
5. France	120	116	123	359
6. Germany (up to 1964) From 1968, two separate teams:	98	127	118	343
East Germany	29	32	30	91
West Germany	18	21	26	65
7. Italy	106	88	91	285
8. Hungary	92	83	100	280
9. Finland	80	70	95	245
10. Australia	57	50	51	158

Name	Gold	Silver	Bronze	Total
11. Japan	49	55	43	147
12. Switzerland	36	51	47	134
13. Netherlands	39	40	43	122
14. Denmark	27	47	45	119
15. Canada	22	37	48	107
16. Poland	23	27	50	100
17. Norway	39	29	30	98
18. Czechoslovakia	33	35	29	97
19. Belgium	18	37	29	84
20. Austria	15	23	30	68

World Records in Athletics
(A star against the athlete's name means that her time is awaiting ratification)

Track events	Holder	Time min. sec.
100 yards	Chi Cheng (Taiwan)	10.0
100 metres	R. Stecher (E. Germany)	10.9
200 metres	R. Stecher* (E. Germany)	22.1
220 metres	Chi Cheng (Taiwan)	22.6
400 metres	M. Neufville (Jamaica) M. Zehrt (E. Germany)	51.0
440 yards	K. Hammond (U.S.A.)	52.2
800 metres	H. Falck (W. Germany)	1 58.5
880 yards	J. Pollock (Australia)	2 01.0
1,500 metres	L. Bragina (U.S.S.R.)	4 01.4
1 mile	P. Cacchi (Italy)	4 29.5
100 metres hurdles	A. Ehrhardt* (E. Germany)	12.3
200 metres hurdles	P. Ryan (Australia)	25.7

Field events	Holder	Distance metres
Long jump	H. Rosendahl	6.85
High jump	J. Blagoyeva (Bulgaria)	1.94
Shot	N. Chizhova (U.S.S.R.)	21.03
Discus	F. Melnik (U.S.S.R.)	67.43
Javelin	R. Fuchs (E. Germany)	65.04
Pentathlon (5 events)	B. Polsk (E. Germany)	4,831 points

Badminton
Women's International Championship (Uber Cup)

1957 U.S.A.	1960 U.S.A.	1963 U.S.A.
1966 Japan	1969 Japan	1972 Japan

All England Championships (women) since war

1947	M. Ussing	1962	Mrs. G. C. K. Hashman
1948	K. Thorndahl	1963	Mrs. G. C. K. Hashman
1949	A. Schiott Jacobsen	1964	Mrs. G. C. K. Hashman
1950	Mrs. T. Ahm	1965	Ursula Smith
1951	A. Schiott Jacobsen	1966	Mrs. G. C. K. Hashman
1952	Mrs. T. Ahm	1967	Mrs. G. C. K. Hashman
1953	M. Ussing	1968	Mrs. E. Twedberg
1954	J. Devlin	1969	Miss H. Yuki
1955	M. Varner	1970	E.Takenaka
1956	M. Varner	1971	Mrs. E. Twedberg
1957	J. Devlin	1972	Miss N. Nakayama
1958	J. Devlin	1973	Miss M. Beck
1959	H. M. Ward	1974	Miss H. Yuki
1960	J. Devlin	1975	Miss H. Yuki
1961	Mrs. G. C. K. Hashman		

Lawn Tennis *Wimbledon champions since war (women)*

1946	Miss P. Betz	1961	Miss A. Mortimer
1947	Miss M. Osborne	1962	Miss K. Susman
1948	Miss A. Brough	1963	Miss M. Smith
1949	Miss A. Brough	1964	Miss M. Bueno
1950	Miss A. Brough	1965	Miss M. Smith
1951	Miss D. Hart	1966	Mrs. B. J. King
1952	Miss M. Connolly	1967	Mrs. B. J. King
1953	Miss M. Connolly	1968	(1st Open) Mrs B. J. King
1954	Miss M. Connolly	1969	Mrs. P. F. Jones
1955	Miss A. Brough	1970	Mrs. B. M. Court
1956	Miss S. Fry	1971	Miss E. Goolagong
1957	Miss A. Gibson	1972	Mrs. B. J. King
1958	Miss A. Gibson	1973	Mrs. B. J. King
1959	Miss M. Bueno	1974	Miss C. Evert
1960	Miss M. Bueno	1975	Mrs. B. J. King
		1976	Miss C. Evert

Wightman Cup	1946	U.S.A.	1962	U.S.A.
	1947	U.S.A.	1963	U.S.A.
	1948	U.S.A.	1964	U.S.A.
	1949	U.S.A.	1965	U.S.A.
	1950	U.S.A.	1966	U.S.A.
	1951	U.S.A.	1967	U.S.A.
	1952	U.S.A.	1968	U.S.A.
	1953	U.S.A.	1969	U.S.A.
	1954	U.S.A.	1970	U.S.A.
	1955	U.S.A.	1971	U.S.A.
	1956	U.S.A.	1972	U.S.A.
	1957	U.S.A.	1973	U.S.A.
	1958	Great Britain	1974	Great Britain
	1959	U.S.A.		
	1960	Great Britain		
	1961	U.S.A.		

Records
Greatest number of Wimbledon wins: Mrs. Helen Wills-Moody (U.S.A.), who won the singles title eight times in 1927-28-29-30-32-33-35-38.
Greatest number of titles ever won: 19, by Miss Elizabeth Ryan (U.S.A.) between 1914 and 1934.

Table Tennis
World Champions (women) since war

1947	G. Farkas (Hungary)	1959	K. Matsuzaki (Japan)
1949	G. Farkas (Hungary)	1961	Chiu Chung-Hui (China)
1950	A. Rozeanu (Rumania)	1963	K. Matsuzaki (Japan)
1951	A. Rozeanu (Rumania)	1965	N. Fúkazu (Japan)
1952	A. Rozeanu (Rumania)	1967	S. Morisawa (Japan)
1953	A. Rozeanu (Rumania)	1969	T. Kowada (Japan)
1954	A. Rozeanu (Rumania)	1971	Lin Hui Ching (Formosa)
1955	A. Rozeanu (Rumania)	1973	H. Yu-Lan (China)
1956	T. Okawa (Japan)	1973	H. Yu-Lan (China)
1957	F. Eguchi (Japan)	1975	E. Antonian (U.S.S.R.)

Rowing
University Boat Race
Putney to Mortlake—4 miles, 1 furlong, 180 yards. Oxford have won 52 times, Cambridge 61 and there has been 1 dead-heat (in 1877).

1946	Oxford	1962	Cambridge
1947	Cambridge	1963	Oxford
1948	Cambridge	1964	Cambridge
1949	Cambridge	1965	Oxford
1950	Cambridge	1966	Oxford
1951	Cambridge	1967	Oxford
1952	Oxford	1968	Cambridge
1953	Cambridge	1969	Cambridge
1954	Oxford	1970	Cambridge
1955	Cambridge	1971	Cambridge
1956	Cambridge	1972	Cambridge
1957	Cambridge	1973	Cambridge
1958	Cambridge	1974	Oxford
1959	Oxford	1975	Cambridge
1960	Oxford	1976	Oxford
1961	Cambridge	1977	Oxford

Swimming *World records (women)*		*Time*
Event	Holder	min. sec.
Freestyle		
100 metres	K. Ender (E. Germany)	58.1
200 metres	S. Gould (Australia)	2 03.5
400 metres	S. Gould (Australia)	4 19.0

Event	Holder	Time min. sec.	
800 metres	K. Rothhammer (U.S.A.)	8	53.7
1,500 metres	S. Gould* (Australia)	16	56.9
Backstroke			
100 metres	K. Muir (South Africa)	1	4.5
20 metres	M. Belote	2	19.2
Breaststroke			
100 metres	C. Carr (U.S.A.)	1	15.6
200 metres	C. Ball (U.S.A.)	2	38.5
Butterfly stroke			
100 metres	K. Ender (E. Germany)	1	03.1
200 metres	K. Moe (U.S.A.)	2	15.5
Individual medley			
200 metres	K. Ender* (E. Germany)	2	23.0
400 metres	A. Franke (E. Germany)	5	01.1

Cross-Channel Swimming
Only woman to swim both ways: Florence Chadwick
(U.S.A.): 1951, France to England, 16 hr. 22 min.
1953, England to France, 14 hr. 42 min.
1955, England to France, 13 hr. 5 min.
Fastest crossing by a woman: 9 hr. 36 min., by Lynn Cox (U.S.A.)
1973, from England to France.

Show Jumping
Leading Show Jumper at Horse of the Year Show

Year Horse	Owner	Rider
1949 Finality	Mr. J. Snodgrass	Pat Smythe
1950 Sheila	Mr. Y. Makin	Seamus Hayes
1951 Eforegiot	Hon. Dorothy Paget	Curly Beard
1952 Snowstorm	Mr. R. Hanson	
1953 Red Admiral	Mr. A.H. Payne	Alan Oliver
1954 Earlsrath Rambler	Capt. J. Palethorpe	Dawn Palethorpe
1955 Sunday Morning	Mrs. N. Cawthraw	Ted Williams
1956 Dumbell	Mrs. N. Cawthraw	Ted Williams
1957 Pegasus XIII	Mr. L. Cawthraw	Ted Williams
1958 Mr. Pollard	Mr. J. King	Pat Smythe
Jane Summers	Mr. T.H. Edgar	Ted Edgar
1959 Farmer's Boy	Mr. H. Smith	Harvey Smith
1960 Lucky Sash	Miss A. Barker	David Barker
1961 Mayfly	Mrs. H.H. Bibby	Carole Beard
1962 Wildfire	Mr. F. Broome	David Broome
1963 Vibart	Andrew Fielder	Andrew Fielder
1964 Royal Lord	Mr. G. Hobbs	George Hobbs
1965 Sudden	Miss M. Coakes	Marian Coakes
1966 Vibart	Andrew Fielder	Andrew Fielder

1967 Harvester	Mr. B. Cleminson	Harvey Smith
1968 Vibart	Andrew Fielder	Andrew Fielder
1969 Uncle Max	Mr. T. H. Edgar	Ted Edgar
1970 Stroller	Mrs. D. Mould	Marian Mould
1971 Pitz Palu	Mr. & Mrs. L. Cawthraw	Alan Oliver
1972 Psalm	Mr. & Mrs. N. Moore	Anne Moore
1973 Sportsman	Esso Petroleum Company	David Broome
1974 Salvador	Harvey Smith	Harvey Smith
1975 Philco	Harris Acrilan Carpets	David Broome

Racing

Derby (run at Epsom, 1½ miles)		*Grand National (Aintree, 4 miles, 856 yds)*	
1946	Airborne	1946	Lovely Cottage
1947	Pearl Diver	1947	Caughoo
1948	My Love	1948	Sheila's Cottage
1949	Nimbus	1949	Russian Hero
1950	Galcador	1950	Freebooter
1951	Arctic Prince	1951	Nickel Coin
1952	Tulyar	1952	Teal
1953	Pinza	1953	Early Mist
1954	Never Say Die	1954	Royal Tan
1955	Phil Drake	1955	Quare Times
1956	Lavandin	1956	E.S.B.
1957	Crepello	1957	Sundew
1958	Hard Ridden	1958	Mr. What
1959	Parthia	1959	Oxo
1960	St. Paddy	1960	Merryman II
1961	Psidium	1961	Nicolaus Silver
1962	Larkspur	1962	Kilmore
1963	Relko	1963	Ayala
1964	Santa Claus	1964	Team Spirit
1965	Sea Bird II	1965	Jay Trump
1966	Charlottown	1966	Anglo
1967	Royal Palace	1967	Foinavon
1968	Sir Ivor	1968	Red Alligator
1969	Blakeney	1969	Highland Wedding
1970	Nijinsky	1970	Gay Trip
1971	Mill Reef	1971	Specify
1972	Roberto	1972	Well To Do
1973	Morston	1973	Red Rum
1974	Snow Knight	1974	Red Rum
1975	Grundy	1975	L'Escargot
1976	Emperey	1976	Rag Trade